Barbara thirty years and has had hundreds of short stories and articles published by magazines. She has previously had two non-fiction books published, written jointly with her husband, Robin Dynes. Barbara is currently a columnist for *Writers' Forum* magazine and has worked as a creative writing tutor and lectured in the subject for many years.

MASTERCLASSES IN CREATIVE WRITING

Barbara Dynes

With love and special thanks to my husband, Robin, for his invaluable help and support.

To Derek and Kevin, from their 'computer-dumb' Mum, with love. And to all my writing students and friends, from whom I have learned so much.

Constable & Robinson Ltd
55-56 Russell Square
London WC1B 4HP
www.constablerobinson.com

First published in the UK by How To Books,
an imprint of Constable & Robinson Ltd., 2014

A copy of the British Library Cataloguing in Publication
Data is available from the British Library

ISBN 978-1-84528-511-1 (paperback)
ISBN 978-1-47211-003-9 (ebook)

Printed and bound by CPI Group (UK) Ltd, Croydon, CR0 4YY

13 5 7 9 10 8 6 4 2

CONTENTS

INTRODUCTION

Welcome to the world of creative writing. Whilst teaching the subject, I became aware that students often had their own individual 'stumbling block' regarding certain aspects of writing. For instance, some could not grasp viewpoint, some were conscious of using stilted dialogue or adding corny endings. Students suggested that a 'dip into' a reference book that pulled no punches and concentrated on the nitty-gritty, could be the answer.

So here is that 'dip into' book, where you can go straight to your particular problem. But I hope that you will also gain confidence and enjoyment from the other 'lessons' which, together with the exercises, are aimed at getting new writers into print and improving the work of those already published. The exercises should also be fun to do if you are writing for pleasure.

The approach that authors take – the attitude they have towards writing – is so important. Over the years I have had brilliant students who, sadly, were unwilling to do the hard work required, and not so brilliant ones who, fantastically, would slog away at it. Guess which are successful today …

There are no real 'rules' in creative writing, but you do need to learn the basics and these lessons are aimed at keeping you writing, in spite of those 'blocks'. There is nothing more satisfying than finishing your own story or novel, so get down to it.

Read the good authors … and keep writing!

AUTHOR'S NOTE
Throughout the book, please read 'he' to encompass both men and women. No sexism intended!

SECTION ONE:
GETTING STARTED

(1)
HAVING THE RIGHT ATTITUDE

Attitude is everything! Anyone, given a surge of enthusiasm and a brilliant idea, can start writing a novel or a story. But lack the right attitude towards your creation and it will never get finished. Writing can be fun, enjoyable and wonderful therapy. It can also, like everything else worth doing, be surprisingly hard work.

Before you start to write, spend a few moments thinking about what you are about to do. Why do you want to do it? For fun ... just to see if you CAN do it ... in order to create something ... because you've always loved words? Or maybe you're deadly serious and hope to sell your work? Whatever, even if you've never written anything creative before, you need to get into a positive frame of mind about it and be determined to finish what you start. The '*I'll-just-scribble-a-few-words-and-see-where-they-take-me*' attitude is not always good. OK, it gets you started, but your first surge of enthusiasm is likely to peter out ... and yet another creative piece comes to nothing.

Whatever stage you are at, be positive about any writing you attempt. Giving yourself a deadline (a completion date) and sticking to it helps enormously. You need to make a solid commitment about your writing: you are no 'dabbler', you intend to produce a complete story or a whole novel. Even if you are doing it just for fun, you'll get much more satisfaction from your creation if you manage to finish it. So, remember: attitude is everything!

MASTERCLASS EXAMPLE
I don't know anything about inspiration because I don't know what inspiration is – I've heard about it, but I never saw it.

(William Faulkner)

TOP TIP

Think you're not in the mood? No matter – sit in front of your computer and write something. Anything! Keep going, then read it back. Among that jumble of words you will find something that interests you. Leap on it – it's a start!

HAVING THE RIGHT ATTITUDE – THE MAIN POINTS
- Be positive
- Give yourself a deadline
- Finish the piece and enjoy the satisfaction of producing something creative

Exercise 1

Fill in the following:

Why do you want to write? (to sell your work, for fun, therapy)

MY COMMITMENT IS:
I shall start my story on _____
I shall write at least _____ *words every time I go back to it*
I shall finish my story by _____
Signature _____

Now, sign your statement … go on! You have made a commitment. By signing it you are reminding yourself how absolutely committed you are. This way, you WILL keep to it!

Exercise 2

Sit in front of the computer and just write. Write any old rubbish – about the colour of the wall over the top of your machine, the electricity bill on your desk, waiting to be paid. Supposing you didn't pay it? You would have no lighting, no heating. You'd have to go to a café to get warm; who might be in that café …

Just keep writing anything. I guarantee some spark of an idea will emerge!

(2)
FINDING AND RECOGNISING IDEAS

Are you one of those writers who are never short of an idea? Some people's notebooks or computers are full of them. These lucky folk have so many ideas they don't know which to use first. If you find good ideas are a rarity, you'll be envious of that first group.

Well, take heart! Those writers teeming with ideas are not always the ones who produce the most work. The danger is that they can start on one project, hit a snag and, whilst searching for a solution, recall that other brilliant idea just waiting to be worked on ... and abandon the first. Some authors never finish anything, which is a sad state of affairs. It is tempting to move on to another – perhaps more exciting – project, but not very productive if the first piece never gets finished. Usually, those who find ideas hard to come by do not have this problem. They are so relieved to get a rare, workable one that they tend to stick with it to the end!

Content
When you get an idea for a short story, make sure that the content will suit the form. If your idea is too complicated, with lots of twists and turns, it might be novel material. How much time does it cover? A short story of around 1,000 words is better told over a short period of time, say a day, or a couple of hours. Readers don't want to jump long stretches of time in so short a story. Before you begin to write, you need to think about where you might sell it. Short stories are most often published in magazines. If it's for a particular magazine, you must angle the idea to suit it, or perhaps you know of a market online which might be interested? Or you might decide to aim for a competition, particularly if the story is a bit of a quirky, weird conception and comes

7

under a genre which most magazines will not touch. You will find lots of open competitions in writing magazines, newspapers and online. These offer far more freedom and choice of subject.

If your idea is for a novel, you will have more scope when it comes to marketing it. But, having said that, you do need to think about genres. Does your idea fit into one? Not really, you say. Could you possibly change the concept of it so that it would fit? OK, it's your baby and you don't want to alter anything; of course you don't. But fitting into a genre is not half as bad as it sounds. You can still write the novel you want to write, but you might need to change the format a little. If you do that – so that it fits into a genre – you'll have far more chance of selling it. And getting it out there for people to enjoy has to be better than sticking it in a drawer at home (see (48) 'Checking on Market Study').

Where to find ideas

Ideas are all around us, people say. True. It's just that a lot of us don't recognise their potential. There are sources such as newspapers, TV, radio and the Internet, but often our best ideas come from our own experiences and the people we meet every day. What we need to do, as we go about our daily lives, is to keep reminding ourselves that we are writers. And everything we experience, everything we feel, is possible material. Keep asking yourself: can I use this in my fiction? Could I twist it, add something to it and use it? Get out your notebook (if you call yourself a writer you'll always carry a notebook) and scribble down a few necessary words as a reminder. Don't make the mistake of thinking, 'I'll remember that.' You won't.

One important point to bear in mind: an idea is *not* a plot. It is only the start of the process. Don't think that because you've come up with a great idea you are ready to start your story or novel. That idea will need developing into a substantial plot – it craves extras such as obstacles and complications heaped on top of it before the storyline can build up to a climax. (See (3) 'Developing a Plot'.)

MASTERCLASS EXAMPLE

(P. D. James recalls what sparked off the idea for her novel Devices and Desires*)*

I went to Southwold in Suffolk and remember thinking that the sea hadn't changed in a thousand years. And then I just looked north and saw this great power station overshadowing the headland and began thinking ...

I asked myself, Who is doing the murdering? Why? Where? When? Will it be someone from the power station? What are the motives?

She goes on to say she moved the setting into Norfolk, began to make copious notes – using fifteen notebooks – and read several books and pamphlets about nuclear power.

(excerpt from *Writers on Writing* by Alison Gibbs)

TOP TIP

That idea you have, is it original enough? Let's face it, most ideas have been used before. Do some work on it. Can you find a new angle or twist – one that will suit your intended market?

FINDING AND RECOGNISING IDEAS – THE MAIN POINTS

• Will your idea suit your intended market or genre?
• An idea is not a plot. Your idea will require developing into one
• Carry a notebook – and use it

Exercise 1

Pick up a newspaper or magazine, study it and don't put it down until an article or story sparks off an idea that you could work on for a short story or novel. Write down the idea.

Exercise 2

Devise an idea from the following character:

Eccentric Cassie, dressed in layers of old clothes and a long, tatty skirt, her unkempt hair to her waist, wanders around a supermarket. She has no trolley, no basket. What is she doing there?

(3)
DEVELOPING A PLOT

To plot or not to plot? Some writers cannot move forward without knowing where they are going; some dream up a really intriguing character and their entire story stems from him or her. They build their plot around that main character. Others like to work straight from an idea and see where it takes them.

Whichever method you use, remember that a germ of an idea does not constitute a plot. The plot is the detail of what happens in the story and has to be developed from that idea. Don't make the mistake of beginning the story or novel immediately. Do that and you could find that the whole thing fizzles out; you tried to stretch out an idea and create a complete story from it. The plot emerges 'watery' and far too thin – there is no substance. A proper plot is essential. Is it, you say? Some 'literary' short stories, for instance – particularly classical ones – often seem to contain little or no plot. But the majority of writers want to sell their work commercially. And those stories will require a plot in some form or another.

If you are writing a novel of, say, 100,000 words, it is nearly impossible to devise a detailed plot and stick to it. As you write, your story is almost bound to lead you off in a different direction from how you originally planned it. Having said that, we've all heard of authors who plot meticulously and never deviate. It seems to depend on personality – the cautious types amongst us seem to plot first and the impulsive ones just press on regardless.

Working from a plot
The biggest advantage with plotting first is that you know roughly where you are going from the start. You have the confidence of

knowing that you have worked out enough obstacles and complications to pile on top of your original idea and have a satisfactory ending. Of course, you might not stick rigidly to this plot – you'll probably change it around, alter it, add to it or whatever. As you write you might see a better way to tackle the situation, but at least you will have a skeleton plan. It's a kind of insurance, a backup, and I believe – especially for beginners, who have enough to think about when they are first learning to write fiction – it helps to have this reassurance. If you work straight from the idea and your rejections are coming back marked 'plot too weak' or 'too complicated', try working the story out first. It could be the answer.

One disadvantage of plotting is that the process may seem a bit technical and, indeed, not so much fun. Also, you lose a certain amount of spontaneity. But then a well worked-out story has a better chance of selling. And an editor's cheque is very welcome …

Working out your short story plot

The amount of obstacles and complications you add to your initial idea depends on the length and tone of your story. Your initial idea usually constitutes your main problem. After which, depending how strong that problem is, you will probably need other obstacles to add to it, even in a really short story of around 1,000 words. All the way through you are aiming to hold the reader back from the solution – you need to keep him in suspense as to the outcome right until the very end. So, depending on the length, you need enough trauma. Let's say, as an example, your story is to be around 2,000 words. Think of your plot in steps as shown in figure 1: Plot Stairway.

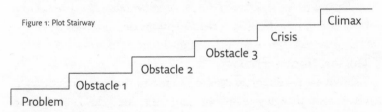

Figure 1: Plot Stairway

If you imagine your story going up, as in the 'plot stairway' example, you will automatically concentrate on building the story, together with the necessary tension, to its climax. Remember that this is a plot plan for a 2,000 word story – you will not always need as many obstacles, depending on the content and how long it is. Also, don't forget that each obstacle does not have to be a massive incident – it can be a tiny emotional crisis. What is important is to be aware that you almost always need more than just the one problem.

Working out your novel plot

In a 100,000 word novel, the tone and pace will be entirely different. Try plotting it out roughly. Down the left-hand side of a notebook or on the computer screen, write chapter numbers 1 to 30, leaving a few lines between each. Allowing for each chapter to pan out to around 2,500 words, the idea is to fill the spaces with anything that might possibly happen – dramatically or otherwise – anywhere along the plan.

Example:

- *Chapter 1: Child is missing. Parents divorced. Father alcoholic, mother distraught.*
- *Chapter 2: Police*
- *Chapters 3,4,5,6, blank*
- *Chapter 7: Girl found. Mentally disturbed.*
- *Chapter 8: Mother looks for kidnapper*
- *Chapters 9, 10, blank*

And so on. You may be devoid of ideas right up until Chapter 30 which, hopefully, you can fill in. What you will find, as you scribble away, is that one thing will lead to another and you will be able to fill in far more gaps than you originally thought. Anyway, you will have some sort of foundation.

This is a very rough calculation. Whatever plot you start with, you will probably change it out of all recognition when you actually write the book. The length of chapters, for instance, will vary tremendously – some short, some long – and that's fine. The 2,500 word count is just for this exercise.

Sub-plots

A sub-plot – which often involves minor characters – is the less important background story; the one that is happening parallel to the bigger one. You might not need a sub-plot for your particular genre. For instance, a romance, with its strong emotional story and characters, will often stand alone. But should you be writing a lengthy thriller, you may decide to weave in a sub-plot as an intriguing extra. A gory murder might benefit from a contrasting lighter story – perhaps one about relationships – as a 'relief' from the heavier content.

If you're really stuck at the idea stage and unable to move forward, Rudyard Kipling had some wise advice:

I keep six honest serving men
(They taught me all I knew);
Their names are What and Why and When
And How and Where and Who.

Use the six serving men - apply them to your idea. Question everything and don't dismiss anything that might help your story. Write it all down. You'll soon have a plot!

MASTERCLASS EXAMPLE
Let everything on stage be just as simple as in life. People dine, just dine, but at that moment their happiness is being made or their life is being smashed.

(Anton Chekhov)

TOP TIP
Predictability – the reader able to guess the outcome – is one of the main reasons for rejection. Added obstacles help here – readers are less able to guess what will happen.

DEVELOPING A PLOT – THE MAIN POINTS

- Get the balance right. Make sure you match the number of obstacles to the length of the story
- 'Obstacles' can be just tiny emotional glitches
- In a novel, remember that the reader might appreciate a lull in the midst of endless action

Exercise 1

From the following short story situation, build a plot along the 'stairway' lines shown earlier. You will need to think of more traumas to add to the initial one. The story is to be around 1,500 words so you should need just the two obstacles.

A young divorced mother has fallen for her daughter's teacher. They have not long moved to the area and she knows nothing about him. The initial problem is that the daughter does not like the teacher …

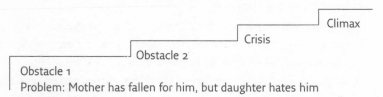

Climax

Crisis

Obstacle 2

Obstacle 1

Problem: Mother has fallen for him, but daughter hates him

Exercise 2

A man meets a girl at evening class. They are both single, he seems pleasant and she agrees to go out with him …

So it's all very nice; a bit too nice! With no hitches, it won't make a story. Work out a plot, adding the necessary obstacles. The first problem will have to come in pretty quickly, before you bore your readers! You could start it on the first date. Maybe he shows a sinister side …

(4)
SUMMING UP YOUR THEME

'Theme?' you say. 'Oh, dear; I haven't got one!'

Don't panic! It's quite usual for a writer, especially a beginner, not to have given 'theme' a thought. Also, if you are writing a novel, this aspect might not emerge for ages, particularly if you are a spontaneous writer who begins without too much idea of where he is going. Nevertheless, it is important that a theme does present itself some time. And it is also important that, when you've finished your story or novel, you can sum up the theme in one sentence.

What constitutes theme?

Theme is an observation of life; the way you, the author, interpret life through your story. Often this emerges as a subject that you feel strongly about – one you feel comfortable about exploring.

One way of analysing theme is to think of it in terms of a proverb. For example, supposing your story is about a burglar. He's been robbing houses for years, but this lovable rogue meets a nice girl and, by the end of your story, he's realised that he can have a better life by getting an honest job. A corny plot, but it serves the purpose. You could sum up that story by declaring 'honesty is the best policy'. And there, in a nutshell, is your theme. You might ask why you need one. Well, it gives you your reason for writing in that particular way. What you are doing is making an observation about living, and your story will be all the more solid for having a strong theme. It is the reason why you are telling your story. You are saying something important through how your characters act and react; also through what they say within the situations, settings and atmosphere you put them in. All of that contributes to theme.

As you write, the theme might be there at the back of your mind, but you are not 'spelling it out'. You are concentrating on what your characters are doing and saying – what is happening at that present time in your story. The action will be a string of events closely knitted together. The thread that connects them is the theme; a sort of invisible thread which holds the story together and runs all the way through the book or short story.

The reader might not think about it as he reads, but afterwards, when a pal asks him what the book or story was about, he will sum it up – and often surprise himself by stating the theme. He had been so involved in the story he'd not been aware of what the writer was getting at. But he'll feel satisfied when he realises that you – the author – have *said* something through writing that story or novel. The theme is the central force of the story.

Short story themes

If you are aiming for publication you will already be aware of the importance of market study. But it is worth mentioning that, if you have a particular theme in mind, make sure that it is suitable for your intended magazine. If that magazine's tone is against the break-up of marriages and frowns on adulterous love affairs (yes, such magazines do still exist today), a story that ends up supporting such events is doomed, however well it is written. Editors are forever harping on about wanting something different, fresh and original for their magazine. Yet that 'different' material still has to be within the magazine's own boundaries; it must suit their readership. You have to find a new take on what is acceptable to that publication. The editor is only concerned with pleasing his readers – the people paying money for the magazine – so study it and see which themes are taboo.

MASTERCLASS EXAMPLE
It is a truth universally acknowledged, that a single man in possession of a good fortune must be in want of a wife.

(from *Pride and Prejudice* by Jane Austen)

(In this example, Jane Austen sums up the theme of her novel in the first sentence.)

TOP TIP

Beware of 'preaching' to your reader via your theme and don't go over the top with it. Let it emerge in a subtle way.

SUMMING UP YOUR THEME – THE MAIN POINTS

• Theme is your observation on life, shown through your storyline
• Theme is an invisible thread running through the novel or story
• Choose a theme which really interests you

Exercise 1

Pick one of the following proverbs and devise a plot around that theme:

1. *Birds of a feather flock together*
2. *You can't teach an old dog new tricks*
3. *The grass is always greener on the other side*

Exercise 2

Choose a short story from the latest copy of the magazine you intend to write for. Note the theme. Write your own story, using that theme. (Absolutely NO copying any part of it!)

(5)
CHOOSING YOUR CHARACTERS' NAMES

How many of us get our idea, work out a plot – if we are so inclined – then bang on with the story, having given no thought to naming our characters? 'Oh, Jane will do,' you say, Jane being the first name that comes to mind. But, hold on! Do that and you are missing an opportunity to add to the quality of your writing. It is really important to choose the right name for your character – especially their first name. For one thing, it is the first means of characterisation in a story – the main character is usually named directly they are introduced. What you choose to call him or her will often depend on their:

- age
- race
- dominant character
- background

Now, you may decide that your hero is to be different, perhaps a bit eccentric. In which case you might ignore the above and go completely against those traits. You could be writing humorously and need to contrast character with, say, background. Strange or unusual names can be used to great effect, especially when given to odd characters and contrasted with a run-of-the-mill background. But, in general, because it helps so much towards characterisation, authors tend to pick a name to suit the type of person they are about to portray.

Get it right before you begin
Let's say an author gives her character a random name. She calls her Keira. Maybe she's always liked it. She is some way into the story

and Keira has really got 'under her skin'. The character has come alive to her. Then someone points out that 'Keira' is too contemporary a name for a sixty-year-old and she realises that she must change it. She is understandably horrified: 'But she *is* a Keira!'

It can be very disconcerting to change a name when you are well into the story; try as you may, you will have a different concept of that character. So get it right before you start. Surnames are different; you can have fun with them. Yet you still need to consider background, religion, etc.

Another point to think about when choosing first names is to avoid having two sounding alike: Alison and Alice or Jack and Jake, for instance. OK, you might have painted their characters so well that readers do not get muddled. Fine! But clarity is important. There are so many contrasting names to choose from, why use same-sounding ones with the same initials? A Katie, too, is better paired with an Amanda than with a Tracey. Katie and Amanda *sound* different to start with. So you are well on the way to characterising them already. You might think that is going a bit far, but not if it helps sell your work!

Assuming you have established the sex of the character, the main things to think about before choosing a name are:

- the type of person
- the age of the character
- his or her family background

The type of person

If you have thought about your story or novel, or perhaps roughly plotted it, you will probably have a good idea of your main character's personality or the sort of person he will develop into. In that case it will be easier to choose a suitable name for him. That is, of course, if you want a conventional name.

Everything depends on the tone of the story you are writing. In general, an ordinary working family from, say, fifty years back, would probably not bestow unusual, fancy names on their children. But it is a fact that most of our favourite fictional characters have memorable names. For example, Scarlett O'Hara and Rhett Butler in *Gone with the Wind*. 'Scarlett' might be popular now, but it was rarely used then, and 'Rhett' is a very unusual name. Author Margaret Mitchell created two really strong characters in that epic story. Yet would they have endeared themselves to us so well had they been called Mary and Bob? Then again, remember Daphne du Maurier's *Rebecca*? Du Maurier used the name of Maxim's deceased first wife as a title. Yet his second wife, the narrator of the book, is never named ...

The age of the character

Characters' names do not always match their ages. Names evolve all the time. A few years ago you could have called a character Hilda or Matilda, for instance, confident in the knowledge that your reader would immediately picture an eighty-year-old woman. But old names have a habit of becoming fashionable again and a four-year-old Matilda is not at all unusual these days. So we have to pick an appropriate name that is *in general* common within that age group. It is advisable to give your character a name that immediately tells the reader what sort of age that character is, rather than choose something startling or unusual. A name such as Jean, Bill, Doreen or Cecil will give you a head start towards characterising a seventy-year-old. (OK, you might know a child of three called Cecil, but, *in general*, it is an 'older' name.) As another example, any Debbies or Sharons you meet today are usually in their forties or fifties.

If you are doubtful about whether you have the right name for the person's age group, a glance at the 'Births, Marriages and Deaths' column in your local newspaper will give you a good idea of who was called what in a particular year. Check that your character's name was popular in the era he/she was born.

Family background

Many names have certain associations for us. For instance, Jim, as an abbreviation for James, was once really popular, but nowadays James usually stays as James or is shortened to Jamie. Often only a James from the older age group is called Jim. Jim was always thought of as a cheerful, down-to-earth matey type, as were Bob, Harry or Alfie. The last two, especially, have been 'reborn' and are popular baby names.

There are always exceptions. That traditional family you create in your story might choose really trendy names for their offspring, but it's unlikely. One thing to take into account is race and religion. Nowadays there are lots of people from abroad marrying into British families, so it is not unusual for a person to have a foreign first name and a name such as 'Smith' as a surname. Or a British first name and a foreign surname. If religion is involved, check your character's full name. For example, if he is a Catholic from Northern Ireland, it would be very unlikely that he is called Henry or William, those being Protestant names. The surname, too, must be researched. Your editor or publisher will not be happy should he receive emails from offended readers!

MASTERCLASS EXAMPLE

'Will you call me a name I want you to call me?' inquired Dora, without moving.

'What is it?' I asked with a smile.

'It's a stupid name,' she said, shaking her curls for a moment. 'Child-wife.'

I laughingly asked my child-wife what her fancy was in desiring to be so called? She answered without moving, otherwise than as the arm I twined about her may have brought her blue eyes nearer to me:

'I don't mean, you silly fellow, that you should use the name, instead of Dora. I only mean that you should think of me that way. When you are going to be angry with me, say to yourself, "it's only my child-wife!"'

(from *David Copperfield* by Charles Dickens)

TOP TIP

Never overuse names, especially in dialogue:

'How's your dad, Pete?' asked Sue.

'Not good,' Pete replied.

'But, Pete, he really should see a doctor,' Sue said.

In that example, *'Pete replied'* can be cut, likewise *'Pete'* in the final line. People do not keep repeating the other person's name in conversation.

CHOOSING YOUR CHARACTER'S NAME – THE MAIN POINTS

- Your main character's name is important. Give it careful thought
- His/her name can help to reveal character
- Consider the type of character, also his/her age and background

Exercise 1

Write down the name of your best friend or someone close whom you know well. Does their name suit their personality? If not, replace it with one that you consider would suit them better. Give your reasons why.

Exercise 2

Pick a name from the following list. Write down how you see that person's age and family background. Now pick another of the names – one that you feel could belong to a character that contrasts with the first. Write a character sketch of that person.

- *Annabel*
- *Joe*
- *Kerry*
- *Sebastian*
- *Godfrey*
- *Terry*

(6)
STARTING IN THE RIGHT PLACE

The beginning of a story or novel is so important that it can give authors a dose of writers' block. You are aiming to grab readers' attention; you know you need some kind of conflict to make them sit up and go on reading. And that is not easy when the whole idea is new and untried – you may not know the characters, the tone or anything else at this stage. So, rather than sit there biting your nails over the beginning, just scribble down or type something vaguely apt and MOVE ON with the story. What you must do, of course – after you've reached the end – is to go back and revise that all-important opening. With the satisfaction that comes from getting the first draft finished, you will feel more confident about giving the beginning a second look.

Grabbing your reader

So, what is a good opening? How about a dead body on the floor, some sizzling dialogue, a couple of really weird characters or a horrifying event? Such drama would certainly make your reader read on! The snag is that grand beginnings like that are not always possible. For one thing, in the case of the short story, we have to consider the tone of the magazine we are aiming at. Most women's magazines, for instance, are not in the business of publishing gory murder stories or terrifying their readers. The sizzling dialogue might be welcome, but does it fit your storyline? If your characters are too eccentric their readers will not be able to identify with them – and identification is really important in a commercial short story.

You'll have more scope in a novel, of course. Surprising or horrifying events can make great openings, but again you have to consider the storyline. You cannot always use a 'shock' type of beginning. But, short story or novel, you do need to grab your reader's attention. And essential conflict at the beginning does not have to be a really dramatic event – it can be just a tiny emotional worry or a mere hint of one. Check your opening. It might not shock or surprise your reader, but it should at least start at the point of conflict or invoke a hint of mystery.

Example:

Debbie stared at the carrots on the supermarket shelf. Dozens of them – some bright orange and tightly packaged, the loose ones a dull, grubby brown. They began to merge into a blur before her eyes and she panicked. She should not have come shopping ...

Carrots might not be as compelling as a corpse, but the above is the opening to a short story, written to suit a women's magazine market. And there is a hint of conflict in that beginning. Is Debbie crying? Why is she crying? Hopefully, the reader will read on to discover her problem. Always aim for some kind of hook right at the start. But remember that a massive hook at the beginning needs a big fish to follow – you must make sure that the style of your first paragraph suits the tone of the rest of your story. A really dramatic opening followed by a quietly told tale will annoy your readers. They will feel cheated, drawn in under false pretences, as it were. In a short story a vivid beginning signals an action-packed storyline to follow. In the novel, however, you have time and space to change the tone; a quiet start does not necessarily mean a slower-paced book. But a hook, somewhere within that quiet start, is essential.

Because of their importance, beginnings cry out for revision. All writing needs revision, of course, but openings especially so. Finish your story first, and then go back and make improvements.

MASTERCLASS EXAMPLE

Hale knew, before he had been in Brighton three hours, that they meant to murder him. With his inky fingers and his bitten nails, his manner cynical and nervous, anybody could tell he didn't belong – belong to the early summer sun, the cool Whitsun wind off the sea, the holiday crowd.

(the beginning of *Brighton Rock* by Graham Greene)

TOP TIP

If you're doubtful where to begin the story, it's a good idea to start it just before a point of change in the main character's life. Even if it is just a small emotional change it creates necessary tension ... and makes the reader read on.

STARTING IN THE RIGHT PLACE – THE MAIN POINTS

- Hook your reader immediately – with an arresting first line or hint of mystery
- Any shock tactics at the start must suit the tone of the rest of the story
- Always go back and revise the beginning

Exercise 1

Write the opening lines of this story, intended for a women's magazine. Plot idea:

Sue, a teacher, married with two children, leads a hectic, contented life. She goes out for a meal with a pal. The pal tells her that she suspects Sue's husband is being unfaithful ...

Where and how would you begin the story?

Exercise 2

Has this piece opened in the right place? How would you begin it? Write an opening paragraph.

Richard was annoyed with the hotel waiters. They'd been ages with his porridge and it was nearly cold. As he sat there spooning the horrid stuff into his mouth, he thought about the phone call. Anne, screeching down the phone that she was leaving him, had really shocked him last night.

(7)
CHOOSING THE TENSE

The tense we use in a story or novel indicates time. The past tense: *He had a regular routine and cooked the same type of meal on the same day of each week,* shows that everything that is about to be related happened in the past and is over with. The present tense: *He panics, aware of the footsteps behind him. In fear of his life, his T-shirt wet with sweat, he breaks into a run,* suggests that the events are happening simultaneously as we read about them.

Note the different types of story. The tone of the first indicates a traditionally paced story and the past tense seems to suit it. The second, with its dramatic action scene, lends itself to grabbing the reader immediately, so it works well in the present tense.

Past tense

This is still the most common and, indeed, the most popular way of telling a story. It has a classic quality to it and is traditionally used by storytellers. Readers are so used to the tense, they barely notice it; they are that comfortable with the past tense. New writers usually find it easier and more natural to use. However, it is wise to consider tense before you begin to write because, after you start your story in the past, it is all too easy to slip into the present tense and not be aware of doing so.

Example:

On her way home from work, Di made for the supermarket. Ian's boss was coming to dinner, so she needed extra milk and a dessert.

'Sorry, miss, we're just closing,' says the guy on the door, smirking as he speaks.

'Just some ice cream, please?' she pleaded, dodging past him. Hurrying towards the freezer cabinets, she grabs a Raspberry Ripple,

then dashes for the check-out. Thank goodness she had made it before closing time.

That won't do at all – both past and present tense are mixed up in one paragraph, making the piece disjointed and confusing. It is better – and clearer – to stay in the same tense all the way through, particularly in a short story. A novel, being much longer, is different. You may decide to change tense to suit the storyline (see 'Multiple Tenses', below). But never do it in the same paragraph, as in the example above.

If you use the past tense it is 'roomier', in that the author can either observe and tell about something or someone from a distance, or get right inside a character's viewpoint. The restrictions and stumbling blocks of the present tense are absent. Flashback, going back in time, need not provide a problem, so long as you make it clear when you are going into it: *He remembered back to the year he had been ill ...* and proceed with what happened then. (See (23) 'Using Flashback')

Past tense can have a certain detachment, a 'holding back', yet the author can still get right into the character's viewpoint – under his skin, as it were. (See (10) 'Understanding Viewpoint')

Present tense
As she walks into the room, she is aware of the silence and hostile stares. 'Hold your head high', she tells herself. She stops in front of Richard, taking his hand. He frowns and pulls it away. She is devastated.

This has the effect of seeming more immediate to the reader, who feels he is right there in the story, immersed in it. It narrows the time distance and works especially well if the story is a) really emotional, b) humorous or unusual, or c) particularly scary. It is even more effective when you use the first person.

Example:

I walk into the room, aware of the silence and hostile stares. 'Hold your head high', I tell myself. Then I stop in front of Richard and take his hand. To my horror, he frowns and pulls it away. I want to die.

First person allows the author to go right into the 'I' person's thoughts and use clichés such as 'I want to die' (which, after all, is how she would think). Humour, too, works well in this tense – again it is better in the first person, especially if you create a quirky character. You can have fun with his thoughts, reactions and dialogue. A scary action story will also work well in this tense. Perhaps someone is being pursued by someone else and you need to get over immediacy and tension:

I crouch down by the wall, gasping for breath. God, he can't be too far behind! Footsteps; heavy and menacing. 'Move girl, now!' I tell myself.

Done in first person, present tense and short staccato sentences, that seems more effective. Try putting that passage in third person, past tense: *'She crouched down,'* etc. Not so scary, is it?

Present tense, whether in first or third person, is not always popular. Some authors – and readers – really hate it, yet if skilfully done it works very well. Modern novelists such as Lesley Glaister and Maggie O'Farrell write in the present tense very successfully. But it is mainly used for short – or really short – stories, when there is less danger of the style irritating the reader. And market study is important. Present tense is taboo to some magazine editors.

Multiple tenses

Changing tense can be really effective, but never do it unless for a specific reason, especially in a short story. Novelists might use this method if, for instance, they are writing in the past tense but need to increase tension or drama during a scene.

Example:

'If Thomas Hardy were still alive …' James droned on with the lecture, wondering if he sounded as bored as his students looked. A noise at the back of the room … the door opening. He looked up.

Cressida. He blinks into the ray of sunlight that surrounds her as she walks in. Perfection … her ice blue dress matches her ice blue eyes. James is completely thrown.

'If Hardy were alive …' he repeats.

Suddenly she turns on her four-inch heels and is gone.

Normality soon replaced her. James stood staring at the bored kids in front of him, then looked at his watch …

You must judge for yourself when, where and if a new tense is necessary. Think about using it when you need to emphasise a change of pace. If you decide to write the story in the present tense, try putting any flashback or explanation of what happened before into the past. Then resume your story in the present tense. Sometimes too much 'present' can get a bit self-indulgent and breathless. A chunk of past tense flashback can throw it into relief and slow down the story for a while.

MASTERCLASS EXAMPLE

She watches while he smiles down at the dog. He throws the ball again, skittering it over the grass, and her longing is more than she can bear. She closes her eyes and his voice whispers between his caresses, saying he knows too well the old woman shouldn't be here. His fingertips are light on her skin, and on her lips when he whispers that it is their secret, that they have always had a secret, since the first day she phoned him up, that everything in the end will be all right.

(from *Death in Summer* by William Trevor)

TOP TIP

Present tense always seems to work better when the story is over a very short period of time, say an hour or two. If the plot stretches to days, weeks, or longer, it can get a bit strained.

CHOOSING THE TENSE – THE MAIN POINTS

• Past tense is more popular and easier to use, especially if you are new to writing
• If you choose present tense, make sure the subject, length, time-span and tone of the story are suitable

- Present tense, with its 'happening now' style, suits emotional, humorous, unusual or 'on the edge of your seat' type stories

Exercise 1

Choose one of the following situations and write the opening paragraph of a short story or novel. Decide which tense – past or present – is best suited to your choice. Will you use first or third person?

1. *An estranged father, dressed as a clown for his son's birthday party, is about to do his act. He is eager to impress his son.*
2. *A daughter, about to be married, is writing a letter to her parents. She will never see them again because they have disowned her over her choice of groom.*
3. *An eccentric old lady, living in chaos, asks a stranger into her home and starts giving away her possessions.*

Exercise 2

Write a very short story – 800 words or so – in the present tense. Include a girl, a dog, a car chase and a jogger. Use third or first person. Even if you dislike writing in the present tense, try it anyway. It is all valuable writing experience.

(8)
ENSURING THE RIGHT LENGTH

What is the correct length for your novel or story? The answer should be: as long as it takes. You need to be able to tell your story comfortably, without any stretching out of the material and, equally, without cramming too much in too few words.

But, before you start, there is one important thing to consider if you are writing for publication – your market. Editors and publishers know exactly what length they want for their magazines and book lists and they expect you to adhere to it.

Novel length

Let's suppose that you are writing in a particular genre and most books in that genre are around 80,000 words. So you need an idea that will develop into a plot to cover that length. Now, seeing ahead like that is not easy – especially if you are new to writing. But consider other novels you've read in the same genre. Pick out one and jot down roughly how many big events, action scenes and traumas the author packed into those 80,000 words. What was the time frame of the novel? Your own storyline will be very different, of course, but studying someone else's plot might help you to pace your own.

You could just plod on with the writing, hoping you'll reach the required target. The snag in doing it that way is the amount of rewriting or cutting you will probably be faced with at the end. If the publishers want 80,000 words they will rarely make an exception for your 100,000, however brilliant the content and writing. What they may do – but only if your work is exceptional and saleable – is to get back to you, requesting that you cut 20,000 words. Which is easier said than done, as the saying goes! A 20,000 cut will mean re-structuring the entire book. But if you end up with just a little over the required length then you won't need to be so drastic. A general tightening up of your prose will usually do the trick. (See (50) 'Being Economical with Words')

At the other end of the scale, if you've tried to pad out the thin storyline of your very short novel to get it to the required length, it will show. Adding unnecessary description, dialogue or non-vital scenes that do nothing except weaken the plot will not work. You may have to think about restructuring and changing the whole story.

Short stories

If you are aiming to sell your work to magazines or online, the length has to be even more exact. If an editor publishes two stories a week, each of them around 1,000 words, it is imperative that you, the author, submit that length. Not 1,300 or 800, but 1,000 – give or take, say, 20 to 30. Don't be too casual about this: 'Oh, it might be 100 words over but not to worry …' Well you SHOULD worry! 1,000-word stories usually fit into one page. If yours is way over that length it probably won't even be considered. There is too much competition today to take chances – your marketing needs to be spot on. So, study the magazine and get the length right – along with the tone, style and content – and you will, hopefully, be on the way to an acceptance.

Competitions

If you are not interested in selling your work – and especially if you intend to write something unconventional that will not suit a traditional market – you can always enter competitions. There are hundreds of short story competitions each year, often with an entry fee, but offering excellent prizes. (Details online or in writing magazines.) They are usually 'open' as regards subject matter – sci fi, horror, romance, crime, etc. – but there is always a length limit. Some competitions require you to put the exact number of words on the manuscript; with others you risk being disqualified if you overshoot the length. Also, if you like to write longer short stories of, say 5,000 words, you are more likely to find a slot in a writing competition than in the magazines. Competitions offer tremendous scope!

Balance

If you find worrying about word count a bit of a bore, try using the process as a balance check. The balance of your story is crucial. When you've finished the first draft, glance through it and see how the plot has developed. Is it reasonably paced – with beginning, middle and end roughly balanced? You can check it through the wordage.

Say your story is 1,500 words long. Where, roughly, do the first 500 words take you to in the plot? Do they cover the beginning (the problem), with the next 500 or so taking up the middle and around 500 for the end? Now, your wordage will probably be far different to this, but this is a rough tool that serves to give you a good idea of the balance of your story.

Supposing, when you do a word count, the beginning (the initial problem) goes way over the first 500 – say to around 800. The middle of the story (the obstacle that adds to your initial problem) adds up to a mere 200 words. And the end (the solution) stretches out to 500 words. In that case, something is wrong with the balance of the story. You might need to prune the beginning, add to the substance in the middle and cut some of the ending. Endings must never ramble on too long. You need a short, sharp finish – especially if there is some kind of a twist.

This is a very rough guide – a lot depends on the type of story – but it does help to give you an idea of the shape of your story.

MASTERCLASS EXAMPLE
I like to get ten pages a day, which amounts to 2,000 words. That's 180,000 words over a three-month span, a goodish length for a book – something in which the reader can get happily lost, if the tale is done well and stays fresh.

(from *On Writing* by Stephen King)

TOP TIP

Don't panic if you find you have gone over the required wordage. Cutting a few hundred words – or even more – can be easier than you think. In nearly every case it improves the manuscript no end.

ENSURING THE RIGHT LENGTH – THE MAIN POINTS
- Take word count seriously
- Padding always shows
- Use a word count to check the balance of your short story

Exercise 1

Write up one of the following situations in EXACTLY 250 words.

A woman steals from a supermarket. She denies doing so to the manager and is aggressive. Her boyfriend turns up and explains that she is mentally ill. The manager lets her off. They drive away … laughing.

A young man, adopted at birth, is to meet his mother for the first time. They arrange to meet in a café. Everything is fine at first, then the atmosphere changes.

(You create your own ending to this one.)

Exercise 2

The beginning of this short story is 71 words in length. Cut it down to around 20 to 25.

Sandra walked down the long, winding lane. The weather was beautiful, very warm and sunny and she felt content. Then she began to worry about what would happen tonight when she met Robert. She told herself not to think about that but to concentrate on the lovely scenery all around her. How wonderful to live in this gorgeous area! Sandra sighed. Suppose Robert was in one of his nasty moods tonight …

(9)
DECIDING WHETHER OR NOT TO PLAN

You might want to do a certain amount of planning before you begin to write your book or story. Which market is it aimed at, how long does it need to be, how much research will you need to do and, importantly, how much time will you be able to allocate to the writing? If you have a deadline you'll need a work schedule that you can stick to. Once you have determined those points, you can begin to plan how you will construct the actual writing of your book or story, i.e. deciding on background, balance, motivation of characters, etc. Planning is intertwined with plotting (see (3) 'Developing a Plot') and also structure (see (22) 'Managing Structure').

Some authors don't ever plan or think ahead, even about their characters. The writer Elizabeth Bowen said: *The novelist's perception of his characters takes place in the course of the actual writing of the novel.* Yet other writers will plan everything meticulously and produce equally good work.

Novel length will usually be determined by the requirements of the genre you have chosen. You will need to study other books in that category and aim for a similar number of words. If you are writing with no definite genre in mind, you will still have to aim for at least 80,000. You might think that a short story of around just 1,500 words does not need much planning. But the opposite is true. Because the story is so brief and concentrated, you need to know where you are going beforehand. Balance and structure are crucial. If it is not solidly constructed the entire story can collapse. A plan will help you decide if your idea is likely to be successful in so short a piece, or whether it would be more suited to a novel.

If you have not planned your novel – decided how much character background you need for your characters, the length required for various scenes, the tone you hope to create – there is a danger that the story will fizzle out or get too complicated after 10,000 words or so. Yet the non-planner might argue that, because the novel is so much longer, there is more time and space to be able to develop ideas as they write.

Advantages of planning

- No rambling away from the main story. Non-planners might create hilarious Uncle Percy in Chapter Five then change the storyline, making poor Percy superfluous to requirements …
- Your story is likely to be better balanced and structured. If your rejection slips state 'ending too rushed', plan in advance and you will avoid such endings.
- Confidence. You know where you are going and are more likely to finish the story or novel.
- If you know your characters before you start, their movements, dialogue and reactions will come more naturally to you.
- Think of the rewriting and editing you will save at the end! No great chunks to cut; a plan will not allow you to put them there in the first place.

Disadvantages of planning

- Planning is hard work.
- A lack of spontaneity.
- Worked out so precisely, the story could come over too 'pat'.

Let's look at the disadvantages in more detail.

Planning is hard work. Yes, it is. The process involves concentrated thinking. How much easier is it to sit and dream up wonderful passages of prose or endearing characters to include in your story – so much more entertaining than working out a detailed plan! But is it not better to put off the dreaming until you've done the hard part – the planning?

A lack of spontaneity. The non-planners say that they have a sense of freedom and wonder that the planner does not. They like to surprise themselves and therefore surprise the reader – and they have a point. Yet it is possible to introduce originality and freshness whilst still sticking to a plan. We should all be aiming to add extra spark to our writing, whichever method we use.

'Too pat' a story. The plan you devise is not infallible. You don't have to stick with it regardless; the chances are you won't be able to, anyway. Particularly with a novel, the story – and the characters – will often suggest different ways to go as you write. There will be things to add as well as to cut. But, importantly, that skeleton plan will be there, in the background, to give you confidence and spur you on. Keep an open mind and change it if necessary, especially if you feel you can improve on your original idea.

If you don't plan and it works for you, then that's fine. But if you are getting rejections, think again. Over the years, I have seen so many stories and novels rejected because of a lack of planning. Their creators were often good writers with original ideas and excellent characterisation, but they had not bothered to think their stories through.

MASTERCLASS EXAMPLE

As to plotting or thinking ahead, I don't in a novel. I let it come page by page, one a day ... try and write out a scheme or a plan and you will only depart from it. My way you have a chance to set something living.

(Novelist Henry Green's views on the subject)

TOP TIP

If you really cannot bring yourself to plan, at least give yourself a little more time to think about the story and characters before you start. You will save a lot of revision later on.

DECIDING WHETHER OR NOT TO PLAN – THE MAIN POINTS

- Planning gives you confidence. You are unlikely to get stuck or give up
- Non-planners probably have more fun!
- Planning cuts editing and rewriting time

Exercise 1

Taking one of the following ideas, work out a rough plan for a very short story of around 500 words, so that you know exactly what will happen. Then write notes on the background you will need, the characters and their motivation and so on.

- *A lost dog*
- *A family feud*
- *A disastrous holiday*
- *Two old enemies meet at a party*

Exercise 2

Create an interesting character. Write a character sketch of that person. Now work out a plan for a short story of 1,000 words, centred round him or her. Make sure you balance the plan, regarding characters, setting, action, etc., to the length.

(10)
UNDERSTANDING VIEWPOINT

This is one aspect of creative writing that appears to confuse and worry writers more than any other. Some people get so anxious about viewpoint that they hesitate to write any fiction. But the more writing you do, the quicker you will understand this part of it. A tip for all those anxious people: just keep writing. It will come, in time, I promise! And once you've mastered the process, you won't look back – it will improve the quality of your writing no end.

What is viewpoint?

Viewpoint is the place or position from which facts are presented to the reader. The author can present them in the first person (see (11) 'Considering First Person'), the third person (see (12) 'Using Third Person'), the omniscient (see (13) 'Understanding Omniscient Viewpoint') and, rarely, the second person or the 'stream of consciousness' style (see below).

When using first, third or second person viewpoint the author can get right inside his character's mind, so to speak; he *is* that person as he writes. By doing this he also encourages the reader to identify with the person as he would if he were alive; understand him, feel for him, care what happens to him and whether he will be able to solve his problem by the end. You, the author, are taking one character's angle on the storyline. The reader experiences everything through that character's eyes.

This is the very essence of writing fiction. You need your reader to feel for the main character and you do this by putting yourself 'under his skin' and staying there. That is pure author identification, which will, in turn, bring about reader identification. The hero or heroine is usually the main viewpoint character – the person whose story it is and through whose eyes it is told – because the author will have devised his plot around that person. In the short story, with its restriction on wordage, events and minor characters, what happens to the principal player is paramount and changing viewpoint is not advisable. There isn't much time or space; readers want to become emotionally involved with just the one character, identifying with what happens to him. And they are more likely to do that if you go straight into his viewpoint ... and stay there.

For example, take this short story plot:

An elderly man's wife has recently died. The man struggles to cope and doesn't appreciate his daughter's help.

It is the man's story so, obviously, it will be better to stay in his viewpoint throughout. Using the most popular viewpoint, the third person subjective (see (12) 'Using Third Person'), it might start like this:

Sam swore under his breath as he went to answer the door. That would be Jenna again, fussing and bringing yet more food. It was kind of his daughter but he just wanted to be left alone to grieve for Maggie.

'Hi, Dad!' Jenna smiled. 'Are you all right?'

Sam gritted his teeth. Of course he wasn't all right! But the poor girl had lost her mother, too; he must remember that. He opened the door wider.

Now, after Jenna speaks, it is tempting to change the viewpoint and describe how *she* feels about the situation. But, as it is Sam's story, it is better to stay with him, inside his mind, as it were. Readers are already sympathising with him about his wife; if you now suddenly put them into Jenna's mind, showing how she feels, it will make the story too jerky and confusing. Readers are involved with Sam and won't want to have to forgo the feelings they have developed for him and his predicament.

If you find staying in the one viewpoint difficult, have you thought of using the first person? OK, you might dislike the viewpoint or it might not suit your idea, but give it some thought. Using 'I' instead of 'he' can make the whole viewpoint issue simpler. When everything is seen from the 'I' person's angle, there can be no danger of jumping out of viewpoint.

Though neither of the following viewpoints is popular with publishers of commercial fiction, they are worth mentioning:

Second person subjective

Example:

You swear under your breath as you go to answer the door. That will be Jenna again, fussing and bringing you yet more food ... (and so on).

Often used when writing a story in the form of a letter or diary (addressing the main character as 'you'), it is rarely used today. The viewpoint can be difficult to maintain and tends to create the impression that the author is intruding upon the reader. Having said that, the £30,000 *Sunday Times* EFG Private Bank Short Story Award for 2013 – won by Junot Diaz, for *Miss Lora* – was written in second person viewpoint. But then Diaz is a prize-winning, experienced author.

The style gives the impression of immediacy and intimacy, lending itself towards an emotional theme. The short story is the ideal form; in longer work all those 'yous' can come over a bit self-indulgent. Yet it has been successfully used in novels. Edna O'Brien's *A Pagan Place,* where it works beautifully, springs to mind. It is perhaps better to consider more popular viewpoints before tackling this rather obscure form, especially if you are new to writing.

Stream of consciousness

Writers such as James Joyce and Virginia Woolf wrote streams of thought 'monologues'. They appear random, imitating how our thoughts jump about, sometimes with erratic punctuation and very long sentences. The writing gives a rambling, unfocused impression, yet must still be coherent.

The end of Joyce's *Ulysses* consists of 62 pages of Molly Bloom's one sentence monologue! Though an interesting form and fascinating when skilfully done by masters such as Woolf and Joyce, publishers today might be doubtful about accepting anything in this viewpoint. But, if your story warrants it, why not give it a go? It is good to experiment with all forms of writing.

Change of viewpoint

Though changing viewpoint in the short story is inadvisable, in the novel – with more time, space and, of course, words – it can be very successful. Though you can stay in the one viewpoint throughout the novel, often an author will go into several viewpoints. Allowing the reader to enter the minds of different characters is intriguing and entertaining and, within 80,000 words or so, the reader has more time to get emotionally involved with various characters.

Your plotline will usually signpost where a viewpoint switch is necessary. Never change without good reason. Bringing in a fresh angle at the start of a new chapter works well; changing viewpoint within short scenes can confuse readers. But should you need to go into someone else's point of view within the same chapter, a gap between the lines will prepare the reader.

MASTERCLASS EXAMPLE

She got up, had a bath, intending to get dressed after it and resume normal life, but the hot water knocked her out. She was barely able to crawl back upstairs and into bed. I'm just resting, she told herself, but fell asleep immediately and slept for two hours, dreamlessly this time.

As soon as he was sure Justine was asleep, Alec went into his study and sat down at the desk, closing his eyes to block out the stale, unfamiliar room. He started to pray ...

(from *Double Vision* by Pat Barker)

TOP TIP

If you've chosen the third person subjective viewpoint, you can only reveal everything that character experiences. Don't be tempted to put in information that he would not know about.

UNDERSTANDING VIEWPOINT – THE MAIN POINTS

• Whose story is it? That person is usually your viewpoint character
• Never change viewpoint without good reason
• Change viewpoint smoothly … and, above all, clearly

Exercise 1

A teenager, his middle-aged mother and his grandfather are standing on a hill overlooking a panoramic view. Write three separate pieces of around 250 words – each from a different viewpoint; going into each person's thoughts.

Exercise 2

Rewrite the following paragraph, which is in three confusing viewpoints. Choose one of the characters and write the piece from just that one angle.

Darren hated Blanche's hair – she'd had it cut far too short and who did Grant, her stupid boyfriend, think he was staring at?

Grant frowned. Who was that menacing-looking bloke eyeing Blanche up and down? Did she know him?

'Hi, Darren!' cried Blanche. Fancy seeing him here, she thought. Embarrassing, to say the least.

Grant glared at Darren who moved towards him, fists clenched, ready for a fight. Guys like Grant did his head in.

(11)
CONSIDERING FIRST PERSON

Writers and readers alike tend to have a 'love or hate' relationship with the first person. 'First person' means that the entire story is told from the 'I' perspective: 'I did this … I did that', all the way through. Some readers, noting that a book is written in this way, will not consider reading it. Anthony Trollope said: *It is always dangerous to write from the point of 'I'. The reader is unconsciously taught to feel that the writer is glorifying himself, and rebels against the self-praise.*

Other writers love this viewpoint, mainly because it seems more intimate and lends itself to a friendly style. When you write in the first person it is as though the protagonist – the 'I' in the story – is writing a diary and talking to you directly. So the reader can identify really closely with him or her.

Example:

I marched into the room, trying to look blasé, but I could tell by Kelly's expression that she was mad at me. Nevertheless, I grinned at her. Never let it be said that I, James Fuller, could be less than charming …

Advantages

- Intimacy. The writer is naturally right inside the character's mind, so the reader will feel closer to him or her, emotionally and otherwise
- Tone. The entire tone of the story will be dictated by the 'I' character, their thoughts and actions. It is, therefore, more likely to be realistic and entertaining
- Viewpoint. The beginner, if confused by the concept of viewpoint, will find writing in the first person easier. He can

become that character and show the whole story or novel from the 'I' angle
- Style. The 'I' person addresses the reader directly, usually in a friendly, confidential manner. Readers feel important – that they are being consulted, as well as entertained.

Disadvantages
- It can be restricting if the whole novel is written in the first person, from just the one character's eyes
- Because the whole story is shown from the 'I' person's angle, he or she must be present in every scene
- It can be a bit claustrophobic. The author can be tempted to indulge in too much reflection and 'deep thought' from the 'I' person
- You need to create a really strong main character who is completely detached from yourself. Using 'I', it is easy to slip into your own mode of, say, speech or habits – and they might be alien to your fictional character.

Why first person?
Instinct will usually tell you whether or not to use the first person. Often, when writers first get the germ of an idea, they will automatically think about the story in the first or third person and stick to that viewpoint. Some authors with a real dislike of reading first person fiction would, understandably, never consider writing in it. A lot depends on the type of story or novel you are contemplating. If it is a romance or relationship story, where emotion and empathy are vital and reader identification is crucial, first person might be better.

If it is a complicated plot, needing several viewpoints to get the story over, you will probably plump for third person. First person would not be practical.

But a lighter theme can come across really well in the first person. Humour, particularly, is really functional in this viewpoint. The main character's quirky ways and speech sound more natural to the reader when he is being carried along in their thoughts, actions, etc. And, though your story might not be exactly humorous, using 'I' will often help to lighten a rather complicated storyline.

If you are doubtful about which viewpoint to use, try experimenting. Write the first chapter – or first page of a short story – in the first person. If you are not happy with the result you can always rewrite the piece in the third. A marvellous exercise in itself!

Changing viewpoint in the first person

A writer can, for example, write a novel entirely in the first person, yet not stay in that particular person's mind all the way through. Each chapter, though in the first person, can change viewpoint. The first three chapters might be from Donna's point of view, but written as 'I'; the next two from Andy's point of view, but again written as 'I'. Using this method, it must be made very clear at the start of the chapter whose viewpoint the author is now in. Heading the chapter with the 'I' person's name is a good method.

Why would a writer do this? Again, it depends on the story. Maybe a really close identity with Donna and Andy has to be established with the reader, because of something that is to happen in the novel. But there needs to be a specific reason to change viewpoint in this way. It can come over as jerky (making the reader jump viewpoints) and confusing. If you fancy doing it as a kind of experiment and for no reason – don't! Some contemporary novelists use both third and first person in the same book. Again, there needs to be a specific reason for doing so.

In his novel, *The Great Gatsby*, F. Scott Fitzgerald used the first person narration method – he had a narrator tell the story of Jay Gatsby. That worked well in that particular story; Gatsby remained an enigma whilst representing the glamour of the Jazz Age.

Male or female

When you write in the first person make sure that as soon as possible you define the sex of the 'I' character. That advice might sound crazy – you, the author, will know whether the character is male or female, but sometimes it is not made obvious to readers and they have to guess. How irritating to discover on the next page that the nervous girl you had begun to identify with is actually a man! Yet it is an easy error to make; we've all done it – brought in our main character, explained their problem and moved on with the story, all without denoting their sex. Remember, your reader is not psychic!

Example:

I sat waiting for the interview, wondering if the other applicants were also this nervous. A couple of girls were actually giggling together. Suddenly I heard my name called. This, then was it …

Is the 'I' there, male or female? It is easily remedied. Insert the name: '*Joan Smith, please!*' Or add: '*My new stilettos were killing me.*' Anything to put the reader in the picture!

MASTERCLASS EXAMPLE

I could have, should have, gone around the world. I should have taken a plane and flown to a different continent, a different climate. I should have done the job properly, changed my name, had my teeth done, a nose-job, siliconed breasts, augmented cheekbones. I should have done hard, definite, permanent things instead of this soft, temporary, half-hearted means of disguise. Only hair. I should have got them to pare my bones, stuff me with something artificial. Something that doesn't feel.

(from *The Private Parts of Women* by Lesley Glaister)

TOP TIP

A downside to using this viewpoint is the tendency to pepper the page with 'I's', which illustrates Anthony Trollope's objection to using first person, as mentioned at the beginning of this section. When you revise your first person story or novel, watch for an excess of 'I's'. Look for ways of cutting the majority of them. It can be done; often by merely rearranging sentences and words:

I stared into my favourite shop windows, not that I could be bothered to buy anything. I was just not in the mood. I'd felt really depressed lately.

Cutting the 'I's':

I stared into my favourite shop windows, but could not be bothered to buy anything. I'd felt really depressed lately and was just not in the mood.

CONSIDERING FIRST PERSON – THE MAIN POINTS

- It establishes a closer relationship with the reader
- Your main character must be strong; you need to avoid author intrusion
- Beginners may find it easier

Exercise 1

Rewrite the following paragraph, changing from third to first person, keeping in Polly's viewpoint but using 'I'. Concentrate on lightening the piece and revealing character by using direct dialogue, thoughts, etc.

Polly had a high-pitched, shrieking voice and put it to good use in the classroom, telling the children jokes and ridiculous stories. She knew she looked ridiculous with her unfashionably large specs, long skirts and clogs. The children were forever telling her so …

Exercise 2

There are seven 'I's' in the following piece. Cut as many as you can by rearranging the sentences, while still retaining the content.

I trudged home from the supermarket with three bags of food, realising I had bought far too much. I had visitors coming – a dreary couple I couldn't stand. Trouble was, I could not avoid having them and I told myself I would just have to get through the evening somehow.

(12)
USING THIRD PERSON

This viewpoint – using 'he' or 'she' when addressing characters – is used by the majority of novelists and short story writers. The most common methods are: third person subjective and third person objective.

Third person subjective
'Subjective' is when you show the story from one person's viewpoint; their problems, emotions, actions, thoughts, etc. Everything is seen through their eyes. It can be easier and less confusing to use just the one viewpoint for the entire story.

Example:

Sheila knocked on Vera's door. Silly to be so scared of her own mother-in-law. The door opened.

'Where's Tony?' Vera asked.

'Busy, I'm afraid,' Sheila answered.

Sheila followed Vera inside. Why wasn't Tony here; he damned well should be, she thought. Nervously, she turned to Vera.

In that short story opening, we are seeing everything from Sheila's angle. We learn of her problem with Vera and her feelings for Tony – we are already getting to know her character. We are anxious to discover how she will solve her problem and want to stay involved with her.

Third person objective
This is when the author does not attempt to get into the mind of the character but looks on to the scene in a more distant way. Third person objective is useful if you want to mention something

unimportant and move swiftly on. Or if you have to bring in something distasteful and need to stand back from the event, rather than write it in detail.

Let's look again at the above example, this time in the third person objective:

Sheila knocked on Vera's door. She seemed nervous. The door opened.

'Where's Tony?' Vera asked.

'Busy, I'm afraid,' Sheila answered.

Sheila followed her mother-in-law inside, then faced her, looking really tense.

There, we are still in the third person, but standing back. We are not right inside Sheila's mind and the reader is not as fully engaged with her feelings.

Using both subjective and objective

Most third person fiction is a mixture of both types of viewpoint. One of the advantages of the third person is that you can slip out of subjective into objective in order to describe a scene or whatever. So you can use both subjective and objective, to suit the story.

Example:

The rain pelted down as the taxi made its way to the theatre. It was getting dark and people clutched umbrellas as they scurried along.

Sid, in the back of the cab, sighed. Show business was all very well but he'd do anything to be heading home instead of having to do this hackneyed play.

In that instance, we start by showing the scene (third person objective) and then go into Sid's viewpoint (third person subjective). Successful stories have been written entirely in the third person objective. But, unless there is a particular reason for doing so, I would advise against it. The story will be 'told' in the coldest sense and there will be little identification with the main character. Is the reader going to care about anyone or anything in such a story? And, if not, are they likely to stick with it?

Whether to use subjective or objective will usually come to you instinctively. Using third person subjective (and adding the objective when necessary) is popular with women's magazines. Editors like their readers to be able to identify emotionally with the main character. It is also popular in the novel – especially in a romance.

If your idea centres round one particular character's problems, hopes, traumas and adventures, it might be better to stay in that person's perspective all the way through. Using that method, you will get your readers more deeply involved with him – laughing and crying along with the one character right to the end.

Changing viewpoint

There is, of course, far more opportunity and time to change from one person's angle to another in a novel. If you do this – still using third person subjective for each – it gives your readers far more scope because they are able to identify with more than one person. Because they are allowed into their minds, readers can discover what one character thinks of the other characters. They can be let into their secrets and plans, ahead of anyone else knowing. However, in general, it is 'safer' to stay in the one viewpoint for at least an entire scene. Some authors stay with the one character for the whole chapter and then change. Beginners, especially, might find that easier and less confusing. But everything depends on the story.

MASTERCLASS EXAMPLE

He gazed into his foam-laced, empty glass. He was feeling his age, whatever that meant. Depending on his mood, *sixty-one* shifted both ways – *only sixty-one* and *my God, sixty-one*. Today it was *my God*. Events had conspired to irritate him, an elderly reaction he knew, but still. First there was the bowel business, or non-business.

(from *The Ex-Wives* by Deborah Moggach)

TOP TIP

If you are worried about whether you have stayed in a particular person's viewpoint throughout, change the 'he' or 'she' words in that particular scene to first person ('I'). You will soon see where you have jumped out of viewpoint.

USING THIRD PERSON – THE MAIN POINTS

- Third person subjective allows the reader to identify with the character
- In a short story, it is generally better to use one subjective viewpoint, going into objective only to summarise or describe
- Any change of viewpoint must be crystal clear

Exercise 1

The following scene is written in the objective viewpoint. Change it to subjective.

Chloe looked glum as she sat on the garden seat alone. She fidgeted uncomfortably in the hot sun and turned away from the colourful roses that Duncan had grown especially for her. It was as though she did not want to be reminded of him.

Exercise 2

The following piece is written from Paula's viewpoint. Rewrite it from Gary's angle, concentrating on his feelings and views of Paula.

'How's your mum these days?'

Paula smiled at Gary as she spoke. Well, she'd had to ask – it was only polite. Yet she dreaded the answer. For a man of twenty he was far too obsessed with his mother. Fair enough to care about her, of course, but there was a limit.

'Not good,' he said, leaning forward over the table. 'She has another cold and I got some medicine for her from the chemist, but … '

He rambled on and Paula stopped listening. His mother should tell him to get a life! But then she loved the cosseting.

(13)
UNDERSTANDING OMNISCIENT VIEWPOINT

Omniscient: knowing everything, so says the dictionary, to explain this rather odd-sounding word. And, indeed, using this viewpoint makes you, the author, an all-knowing, all-seeing, God-like person who can lead the reader into everybody's mind. Up until around the beginning of the nineteenth century, this method of telling a story was the usual practice. It was especially useful for those very long, epic novels that took place over great time spans, involving numerous characters and vast, sweeping landscapes. Today's readers usually demand a more pacey style.

Telling the reader
The key word when thinking of omniscient is 'telling' – use this viewpoint throughout and you will certainly 'tell' your story, rather than 'show' it and, invariably, the story suffers. (See (19) 'Showing Instead of Telling'.) Today, omniscient is not popular; readers prefer to be shown how the character is thinking. That is usually achieved by the author going into one viewpoint at a time (See (10) 'Understanding Viewpoint'), so that readers are able to identify with him and care about him. Omniscient can confuse readers and doesn't allow them to get close to a character.

Example:

Nathan Jones walked into the doctor's waiting room and sat down next to a small girl. He picked up a magazine from the table next to him and pretended to read. Millie Turner, the little girl, was not happy about this – she liked attention, so she decided to annoy him. She tugged at his trouser leg, but he just glared at her. Mrs Turner, the girl's mother – a large lady with a stern expression – tut-tutted at Millie, but at the same time took exception to Nathan Jones. She was of the opinion that children, her precious Millie included, should not be ignored.

Nathan continued reading the magazine. He was a man who did not care much for people. He preferred animals.

Now, if you continue to write like that – in the omniscient, remarking on everyone in general – where is the story? There would need to be a specific reason to comment on all the characters in that God-like way. Maybe if they were all somehow connected? But this is a doctor's waiting room; it is hardly likely. So why use the omniscient?

Because he is mentioned twice, it would appear that Nathan is the main character. If so, would it not be better to go into his viewpoint (third person subjective) to see how he feels ... and stay there?

In the above example, we have gone into the minds of three characters. We know which way they are thinking; they have no secrets. And, in the scheme of things, is that natural? In real life we do not know what is going on in other people's minds – we can guess, of course – but we don't know for certain. Stay in the omniscient all the way and the reader learns everything, which leaves little room for surprise. Ask yourself – would it really be right for my story?

A particular plot

Omniscient could suit a certain type of plot. For instance, supposing you – the author – have several main characters hating (or at odds with) each other and you want the reader to discover how they eventually resolve their problems and come together. You could do this by staying on the outside looking on – 'telling' each person's side of the story in turn. But remember that if you do this – stand right back in order to tell about each character – it will be a 'cold' account, told in a somewhat clinical way.

When you come to revise the story, be strict with yourself. Does it work like this? Might the story benefit more if shown from one of their viewpoints, thereby introducing some feeling and reaction? Change it from omniscient to third person subjective and you will create far more emotional depth.

Unless your particular plot demands it, it is better that you do not tell the story using the omniscient. Readers of today's short stories and novels much prefer to identify with just the one character, going solely into his viewpoint. They do not want to be 'told' about that person in a factual way. Using omniscient viewpoint throughout – with the author as the all-seeing, God-like person looking on to the scene – tends to produce text that is very detached and devoid of emotion. Readers like to feel something – love, hate, anger or whatever – for the characters. That is the reason they read fiction.

Use omniscient sparingly. It can be useful when you want to describe an essential, yet unimportant scene, or when setting the stage for a dramatic situation. This is better done at the beginning of your story, before you go into an individual's viewpoint and begin to involve the reader with him.

MASTERCLASS EXAMPLE

It was 3.35 p.m., Tuesday afternoon, in the State Penitentiary, and the inmates were returning from the workshops. Men in unpressed, flesh-coloured uniforms, each with a number on the back, streamed through the long corridor of A-block, and a low hum of voices rose from them, though none of the men seemed to be talking to anyone near by. It was a strange, unmusical chorus ...

(from *The Glass Cell* by Patricia Highsmith)

(Highsmith says of this opening of her novel: *I was counting on the reader's curiosity about the unusual setting, a prison, to carry him* (the reader) *along. The dreariness of the rhythm is the dreariness of the prison atmosphere also ...*)

TOP TIP

Using the omniscient viewpoint at the beginning of your story or novel can be a way of mentioning someone or something which will be crucial to the plot, but difficult to bring in later. You can forecast a coming event that you don't want your main character to know about.

UNDERSTANDING OMNISCIENT VIEWPOINT – THE MAIN POINTS
- As a main viewpoint, it is rarely used today, but a certain type of story might benefit
- The reader will be unable to identify with anyone, so there will be no real depth of emotion
- It can get irritating and confusing for the reader to be in on everyone's thoughts

Exercise 1
Which of these plot ideas might benefit from the omniscient viewpoint? Pick one, then write the first 500 words of a short story, entirely in the omniscient.
1. Mother and daughter do not get on. The daughter is due to be married and Mother interferes.
2. Two men confront each other in a pub. Both are after the same girl. One knows the other is a womaniser. The womaniser knows that the first man is involved in drugs
3. A man whose wife has recently died meets another woman. He is not interested and is quite rude to her

Exercise 2
Two people are having a picnic. (On the beach? In the park?) Choose a place, then open a story in the omniscient viewpoint, describing the scene in a short paragraph. Now, pick one character and go into his or her thoughts (third person subjective) and write the next paragraph.

SECTION TWO:
DEVELOPING THE STORY

(14)
GETTING TO KNOW YOUR CHARACTERS

Good characterisation is vital. Above everything else, people are mainly interested in people. However good the storyline, readers will stop reading if they feel nothing for the characters. They want to get emotionally involved with your protagonist and identify with him, caring about him or maybe despising him; they need to feel his reactions – his love, hate, sympathy, impatience or whatever – for the other characters. Some authors write a story or novel directly from a character they have created, rather than work out a plot. They allow the plot to develop from that person's actions, personality or whatever. Those authors will probably have done some really hard thinking about their protagonist before they began to write, which is great.

Bringing characters to life

So, what is the best way to ensure that your characters really 'come to life'? By doing a character sketch *before* you begin your story. (That word *before* is very important. Take note of it and you will save yourself a lot of rewriting afterwards.) Write down how characters look, what type of people they are, their weaknesses and good points – anything that comes into your head. Often the most interesting characters are slightly eccentric or 'off-key' in some way. Think about giving your so-called normal person a very loud laugh or an odd way of speaking or maybe he walks with a pronounced limp.

I can hear you thinking: 'Oh, I know my main character – she's tall, twenty-five and a bit arrogant.' But that isn't enough. What does she have for breakfast, is she late or early for appointments, is she a worrier, is her house a tip? OK, you might never use those facts, but knowing more about her than you will use will make her come alive, both for you and your reader. It is the tip of the iceberg theory; you put in only what is necessary to the storyline, yet the important bits are there, under the surface. And, what's more, the story will be easier to write. Learning so much about your character – getting under her skin, as it were – will help enormously with other aspects of your writing.

For one thing, you'll know instinctively how she will think and react to any situation you put her into. You will find her dialogue much easier – her mode of speech, her answers, the way she deals with people. Knowing your character will also help with the plot. As you work it out, you'll be able to judge whether this woman you now know so well would really do what you are about to make her do, speak in that cruel way or be such a 'doormat' to others. Ask yourself, would this type of person really do that? You may need to change some aspect of your plot to make her credible to the reader. But you can only do that if you know your character as well as you would know a sister or brother.

Let's suppose that, earlier in the storyline, you created Nigel as a meticulous bachelor, always early, very tidy and mean with his money. The main conflict is that he's lonely and meets a couple of girls through a dating agency. Of course, you'll need other complications, but the upshot is he ends up with the brassy type who likes a good time and spends money like water. Now, even if he's besotted with her, would a man like that really 'go off into the sunset' with that type of girl? You may say, 'Ah, but he needs to change and she'll help him.' Right, but is the story credible? A lot depends on how well you've got his character across to the reader. Maybe you've created him with depth … he is not really as he seems. Therefore, he is capable of change. The big question is: will your readers believe that? You'll only get them to believe it if you've done a really good job with his characterisation.

In both the short story and the novel it is important that your main character changes in some way – however small – by the end, through what has happened in the story. Even if you fail to do a character sketch, give your viewpoint character some thought – *before* you start to write.

Too many characters

In a short story of, say, 1,500 words, introducing too many characters is a mistake. The reader wants to identify fully with the main viewpoint character and perhaps marginally with one or two others – three at the most. Otherwise you risk confusing the storyline. The shorter the story the fewer 'players' it will take. Needing a lot of characters usually signifies an over-complicated plot. Is it novel material?

In a novel you will probably need a lot more characters, along with a change of viewpoint, but economy here is just as important. Question each person you bring on to the scene. Does eccentric Aunt Dora, created in Chapter Five, really do anything for the story? If not then – sadly – she has to go.

MASTERCLASS EXAMPLE

He had changed since his New Haven years. Now he was a sturdy straw-haired man of thirty, with a rather hard mouth and a supercilious manner. Two shining arrogant eyes had established dominance over his face and gave him the appearance of always leaning aggressively forward. Not even the effeminate swank of his riding clothes could hide the enormous power of that body – he seemed to fill those glistening boots until he strained the top lacing, and you could see a great pack of muscle shifting when his shoulder moved under his thin coat. It was a body capable of enormous leverage – a cruel body.

(from *The Great Gatsby* by F. Scott Fitzgerald)

TOP TIP

Putting a character in a situation opposite to their nature adds drama to the plot. Also, if you find yourself 'making' your character do something, you are on dangerous ground. If you know him well enough you should not have to 'make' him do anything.

GETTING TO KNOW YOUR CHARACTERS – THE MAIN POINTS

- Know your main character thoroughly before you start to write: do a character sketch
- Readers need to identify with the character and feel something for him: love, pity, hate or whatever
- Remember that great characters are often a bit odd!

Exercise 1

As an example, the columns below are filled with the traits of a fictional character. Now think of someone you know and fill in the columns with their character traits. Add other headings as you wish.

Appearance	Strong points	Weaknesses	Likes	Dislikes
grey, frail walks with a stick	loves children generous	terrible temper drinks heavily	sport TV	bad manners dogs

Exercise 2

Pick one of the following characters:

Selina, aged twenty   Jessie, aged sixty-nine   Darren, aged nineteen

Write a character sketch about that person and include the following facts. Is he/she:

- Tidy or untidy?
- Late or early?
- Mild-mannered or aggressive?
- Mean or generous?
- A healthy eater or chips-with-everything type?

(15)
MAKING GOOD USE OF DIALOGUE

Dialogue plays an important part in a novel or story. Though we have all read books or stories that contain little or no actual speech and thoroughly enjoyed them, dialogue can help to bring a scene to life. There are two ways of getting it across. One is when the author just tells us what is said: *Ryan declared that he did not want to go out.* That is *indirect* dialogue. The other – *direct* dialogue – is to let us actually hear Ryan say it: *'I'm not going out, so there!' Ryan declared.* Often it is a case of deciding whether the conversation is important enough to let readers actually hear it, thereby creating a scene. The advantages of using direct dialogue are enormous. It will help to:

- Characterise the speaker
- Move the story on
- Give information
- Break up long passages of narrative
- Dramatise the story

Characterising the speaker

The way your characters speak – how they answer a question, make a statement, react to someone – reveals such a lot about them. No two people speak alike. If you know your characters well, their individual dialogue will be easier to write. Your instinct will tell you how that type of person would answer or react. Make sure each character has a 'voice'. Gruff, moody Stan will speak very differently from timid, demure Mary. Set yourself a test. Cover up all the 'said Mary' or 'said Stan' bits, read through your page of dialogue and see if you can detect who is saying what.

Speech should be individual to each person. We've all read books with lots of separate pieces of dialogue, giving us no clue as to who is speaking, and we have to go back to see who is saying what. This happens when the speech is not varied enough. Also, don't be tempted to over-use names. In real life, people do not keep repeating them: *'Yes, I do know that, Mary,' 'Thank you, Pete.'*

Make it sound natural

You want your dialogue to sound natural, but don't take it directly from actual conversation. Our real life dialogue is often peppered with 'ums' and 'ahs' or we break off in mid-sentence for no reason before attempting to resume what we were saying ... or never finish it at all. Trying to put that down on paper would only irritate and confuse the reader. And, unless giving a lecture, people rarely speak for too long without interruption of some kind. You have to find a middle line – dialogue must seem natural, yet also clear. Read it aloud. All dialogue should be read aloud; the sound of the words will tell you such a lot.

Dialogue can help so much with characterisation, especially in a short story, where space is limited and you cannot go into detail. 'Showing' characters' reactions through speech gets their personalities across. Using indirect dialogue – in other words 'telling' the reader what they are saying – does not.

The novelist Elizabeth Bowen, in her excellent book *Pictures and Conversations*, says of dialogue:

Dialogue is the means of showing what is between the characters. It crystallises relationships. It should, ideally, be so effective as to make analysis or explanation unnecessary.

Moving the story on

If used effectively, dialogue has another use – it moves the story on. Be careful not to waste it – what people say to each other must do something for the story. Too many *'Hello, how are you?'* and *'Terrible weather!'* static-type conversations do nothing for it. Also, use dialogue to create atmosphere. The way one person speaks to another can give a lot away – perhaps create tension between the speakers or reveal a close bond – as well as show progression of the story.

Giving information

What people say to each other can show the reader what is happening in the story or, indeed, what has gone on before. Revealing this in speech can be really effective and means that you don't have to use chunks of narrative to get necessary – but often boring – information over to the reader. Yet it must sound natural. It's tempting to have someone say something out of context merely to remind the reader of a certain fact. Worse still is mentioning things that the people involved would already know – a very clumsy way of getting new information over to the reader.

Example:

'How is your son, Mark, Carrie?' asked Tina. 'I heard he'd been ill since he came back from America. Such a pity he broke up with Kate, but then she was so much older than him and being not yet divorced ...'

OK, that might be a bit over the top, but it makes a point. Carrie, of course, would be aware that Mark was her son, also of his actions, and it would hardly be natural for Tina to repeat it all! If you need to get information over it must be included in a more subtle way, perhaps through thoughts:

'How did Mark cope in America?' Tina said. 'I heard he'd been ill?'

A blessing, really, that Mark had broken up with the awful Kate, Tina thought. Carrie's son was too soft to cope with an older woman – a married one, at that. Not that she would dream of saying that to her friend ...

The second example gives information more naturally, through dialogue and in Tina's thoughts. Doing it that way also aids characterisation – we know how Tina feels about the situation because the piece is seen from her viewpoint.

Breaking up long passages

Pick up a book and turn to a page which is all narrative, with no direct dialogue. Now turn to a page interspersed with loads of dialogue. Which looks the more inviting to read?

Readability is important. Dialogue lightens and brightens every page, so use it wherever possible. Sometimes, of course, there is no opportunity; your storyline lends itself to large slabs of narrative. But take another look at it. Maybe you could break it up by using shorter paragraphs here and there? Keep the readability issue at the front of your mind.

Dramatising the story

Dialogue has the effect of dramatising the story in that it brings your characters to life. It also brings the story to life!

Example in indirect dialogue:

It had to be done. Jodie needed to tell Kevin that his father was leaving them. She sat him down and told him, as calmly as she could, that she and Dad had not been getting on and that Des was moving out. At first, Kevin said nothing, just looked puzzled. Then he jumped up and began to shout that he didn't want his father to go and that he hated her …

Example in direct dialogue:

Jodie took a deep breath.

'Kevin, I'm really sorry about this, but Dad's moving out.'

Kevin just stared at her. Jodie sighed. This was awful.

'Moving out?' Kevin looked puzzled. 'But he can't—'

'You know we've done nothing but row for ages.' Jodie looked away, not wanting to see her son's face. 'It's for the best—'

Kevin suddenly jumped up, his face red with anger.

'No, it's not! I don't want him to go; it's all your fault – I hate you!'

That second example, with the scene written in dialogue, dramatises the whole situation and makes it more vital, as well as characterising Jodie and Kevin.

MASTERCLASS EXAMPLE

'My dear Mr Bennet,' said his lady to him one day, 'have you heard that Netherfield Park is let at last?'

Mr Bennet replied that he had not.

'But it is,' returned she; 'for Mrs Long has just been here, and she told me all about it.'

Mr Bennet made no answer.

'Do not you want to know who has taken it?' cried his wife impatiently.

'You want to tell me, and I have no objection to hearing it.'

This was invitation enough.

'Why, my dear, you must know, Mrs Long says that Netherfield is taken by a young man of large fortune ...'

(from *Pride and Prejudice* by Jane Austen)

(In that passage, from the first chapter, Jane Austen's dialogue does it all. First, it characterises the speakers. Austen doesn't describe Mr and Mrs Bennet till the end of the chapter yet, through what they say – or don't say, in his case – we visualise them immediately. She is flurried, excitable; he a little austere, yet patient with his wife. The dialogue also moves the story on and gives information – Mrs B wants to get her daughters married off. And it dramatises the scene.

The first chapter of the book – three pages in all – is a superb lesson in how to write good dialogue.)

TOP TIP

Use dialect sparingly. Bring in a word now and again, rather than irritate the reader by allowing your character to speak in a broad Scottish dialect, using words that only the Scots would understand. Better to create the rhythm of the speech (Welsh, Irish, etc.) rather than attempt the actual dialect.

MAKING GOOD USE OF DIALOGUE – THE MAIN POINTS

- Make sure each character's dialogue 'sounds' different
- Natural dialogue moves the story on and gives information
- Always read your dialogue aloud

Exercise 1
Characterisation

Rewrite the following situation, putting it into direct dialogue. The girls' different characters should come over through what they say and how they say it.

Tina said no way did she want to go to the party – she hated parties and would not know anyone there. She would rather stay home and read a book. Julie got really irritated with Tina, telling her that she must be mad to miss such a great night out. It promised to be a really wild party – and Julie loved wild parties.

Exercise 2
Moving the story on

Rewrite the following situation, putting it into direct dialogue. Concentrate this time on making sure the story moves on through the dialogue.

As they wait for their children, smooth, well-dressed Roger chats to down-and-out Dan at the school gates. Roger asks Dan what he does for a living. Dan says he's out of work. Roger declares he can help Dan, implying some kind of dodgy deal. The children appear and interrupt them, but Roger needs an answer. Does Dan say 'yes' or 'no'?

(16)
HITTING ON A GOOD TITLE

The title (and the cover illustration) is the first thing to attract attention in the bookshop or online. It is really important, in that it helps to sell your book or short story. The title needs to be dramatic and intriguing to entice people in to discover what it is all about. From the title, the reader should be able to get a good idea of the contents. For instance: *Death in the New Forest* suggests murder, *Love for Sale,* romance and sex, *The Mystery at Hadleigh Hall,* a ghost story, *Escape to Freedom,* adventure.

Authors can have great fun with titles. Currently on the bookshelves is *The Hundred-Year-Old Man Who Climbed Out of the Window and Disappeared* by Jonas Jonasson and *The Woman Who Went to Bed for a Year* by Sue Townsend. Both, I might add, are humorous novels, so the eye-catching titles work because they are in tune with the books' genre: humour.

There are, though, a few pits you can fall into when dreaming up a title.

Misleading titles
In your quest for a really original, exciting title that will make a reader pick up your book, remember that it must reflect the type and tone of the storyline. *A Race Against Time,* for instance, would suggest an action story. The reader might feel a bit cheated if the novel is a 'quiet' book about relationships, with the race against time of the title referring to the heroine's desire to get pregnant before her body-clock runs out. *Murder at Midnight* might make a lover of thrillers swoop on a copy, expecting action and gory death. But if the murder occurred before the story started and it is all about the victim's sister's life – not touching much on her brother's murder – that reader will be disappointed. You do need a good title – but it must promise exactly what the novel or story delivers.

Dull titles

Try to insert an action word or adjective in your 'dead sounding' title to bring it alive. Dull titles like *The Birthday Present, A House by the Sea* or *A Journey* will do nothing to lure people to open your book. On the other hand, *Reluctant Journey* or *Journey to Hell* might.

Clichéd titles

Don't use old sayings or proverbs as titles. Unless you can think up an unusual twist, most, such as *The Tangled Web* or *Winner Takes All,* have been 'done before'. On the other hand, perhaps you have a favourite – not very well-known – poem. A quote from that might never have been used, so you might get a title from it. Or why not think of a well-known phrase then change the wording: *Greed is the Best Policy, One Good Murder Deserves Another?*

Give-away titles

Be careful not to give away any part of your plot in the title; particularly the ending. Also, don't signpost the main character's change of heart through what happens in the story or give any clue as to his fate. *Learning His Lesson, Change of Heart, My Cousin, the Killer* are all 'give-away' titles.

Clever-clever titles

Titles showing how clever the author is are definitely taboo. Your story might be all about dangerous poisons or peculiar unknown plants – you are an expert on them and they make an intriguing background. But don't make the mistake of using a rare plant name or poison as your title. Even if it sounds grand, there won't be many experts who cotton on to it. If a publisher does agree to use it, will it sell? Would you open a book if you didn't understand the title? You couldn't be blamed if you thought it belonged in the non-fiction section …

Short story titles

Those of you who have had short stories published in women's magazines will be rather cynical about titles. Because, however good yours is, you can bet your life that the editor, if he accepts your story, will change it. It is usually within the magazine's rights to change, cut and alter anything they buy from you, so you will have to grin and bear what you think is a terrible title, unless you want to upset the editor …

Though this sounds contradictory, don't just plonk the first title that comes into your head at the top of your manuscript. It is still worth spending time on it. Why? Because, whether it is eventually changed or not, a good title is more likely to jump out from the rest of the pile on the editor's desk. A magazine editor once told me that a title showing flair and originality always made her zoom in on that manuscript. She guessed that the story would most likely be well-written and entertaining. So try to head yours with something 'eye-popping', so long as it suits the tone of the story.

Titles, whether for stories or novels, can be really elusive. Those authors who think of a brilliant one right at the start are lucky. Often they are the 'planners' – they know where they are going with the plot and might even have decided on a theme before they begin. Your theme (see (4) 'Summing Up Your Theme') will sometimes give you your title. Or, if the book is about a specific place you could use that, as George Orwell did with *Animal Farm*. Or maybe it is about a person: *Emma* by Jane Austen and *The Great Gatsby* by F. Scott Fitzgerald are examples. Often authors use a phrase that is used in the story, especially an unusual one, such as *The Big Sleep* by Raymond Chandler. Some of us sit for ages pondering then, in despair, head our work with something that does not do it justice. Give it more time and something better will come to you eventually.

MASTERCLASS EXAMPLES
Catch 22 by Joseph Heller
The Curious Incident of the Dog in the Night-time by Mark Haddon
Standing in Another Man's Grave by Ian Rankin
Before I Go to Sleep by S. J. Watson

TOP TIP

You might not be able to bear showing your completed manuscript to anyone, but at least think about sharing the idea or theme of your novel or short story. Discuss it, preferably with a person who also writes and ask his advice regarding a possible title. A fresh angle on it might very well provide the answer.

HITTING ON A GOOD TITLE – THE MAIN POINTS

- A good title will help to sell your novel or short story
- A dull title will not stand out. Try to include an action word
- Your title must reflect the tone of your novel or story

Exercise 1

Think about the following two plots and suggest an intriguing title in each case.

PLOT FOR A NOVEL

A family of four live in an isolated old house way out in the country. They learn that it is known to be haunted and the mother wants to move out. The husband is cynical about ghosts and won't move. Their five-year-old daughter disappears. They are devastated. Months later she is still missing and their older boy starts behaving strangely …

PLOT FOR A SHORT STORY

A girl is having an affair with a married man. She goes to see his wife, with whom he is not getting on. Then the girl is involved in a mysterious accident. Is the wife responsible?

Exercise 2

Select a book – it could be one you have read recently or maybe one from years back – and think about the title. Could you have come up with a better one to suit that storyline?

(17)
HOOKING YOUR READER WITH CONFLICT

Without conflict you have no story. The conflict is the reason you are telling the story in the first place. You need events to hook the reader – and not just at the beginning. Shocking or intriguing happenings, an air of mystery and lots of tension keep readers reading. There has to be something wrong to keep the story going, even if it is only a slight hitch, or why would anyone want to read on? In the novel, especially, you need strong conflict and motive – physical and emotional – to move the story on.

Beginnings
The *'It was a lovely day and Jane decided to walk through the woods on her way to the shops'* type of opening will not do. 'But', you say, 'she is murdered in the next sentence!' Then you need to cut the first one.

We have all read novels that open quietly, seemingly without that vital hook. But look at them again. Daphne du Maurier's novel *Rebecca*, with its first line: *Last night I dreamt I went to Manderley again* is a case in point. A description of the drive of a house, but with a menacing, atmospheric touch that makes you read on. (See (6) 'Starting in the Right Place'.)

Finding the balance
How much conflict do you need throughout your story? A lot depends on its length – a short story of 2,500 words will require yet more hitches on top of the initial problem, even if that problem seems strong enough to sustain the whole. We've all read stories where one issue is dragged on far too long, with no other diversions

or traumas added – stories which might have worked if drastically cut. The difficulty is finding the right balance – you don't want to cram too much into a 'short short' story. Remember that when you do add a conflict – in a novel or a short story – it does not have to be an enormous event. It can be slight, just a tiny emotional doubt, yet it will serve to add another hiccup, building up the storyline. (See (3) 'Developing a Plot')

All stories need problems. Usually – not always – the longer the story the more you need. Don't forget that sometimes the reader will need a rest from the trauma – a lull in the proceedings before yet more hitches are introduced. And when you do bring in conflict you will need to show motivation – the reason why the conflict happened. Sometimes, especially in a novel, the author has to keep the motivation secret for a while. But, sooner or later, he will need to explain to the reader why the character is behaving in this way.

MASTERCLASS EXAMPLE

Suddenly and simply it had come to him: he had had enough.

Later, he was able to fix the precise moment of that realization, the overhead kitchen light isolating him in a blank world while his hands, twisted by arthritis, fastidiously removed a milky, spear-shaped bone from the fish pie that Mrs Crawford had left for him to warm up for his supper. There was no surprise or shock. Yes, I've had enough, he repeated to himself ...

(the beginning of the short story *A Nice Way to Go* by Francis King)

TOP TIP

When you first get your idea, ask yourself whether that initial conflict will lend itself to yet more obstacles later, especially if you are aiming for a longish short story or a novel. A plot plan consisting of just the one problem that is easily solved will not provide enough conflict in longer fiction.

HOOKING YOUR READER WITH CONFLICT – THE MAIN POINTS
- Always begin with conflict
- You will need additional problems, however slight
- Check that the amount of conflict you have planned suits the length of the story

Exercise 1
Showing conflict, write a gripping first line for the following types of stories:
- *A crime story*
- *A romance*
- *A science-fiction story*

Exercise 2
Rewrite the following piece, bringing in some conflict to grab the reader.

(Plot: Kate learns that her daughter, Zara, is going out with Mike and is horrified – she thinks his family is awful. Get her feelings through – perhaps by changing the dialogue or adding Kate's thoughts.)

'I'm meeting Mike tonight, Mum.'
'Oh, really?'
'He's great – we've loads in common—'
Kate said nothing.
'We're going to Dean's party.'
'Well, don't be too late—'
'Don't wait up. See you!'
Zara slammed the front door.

(18)
USING ACTION TO MOVE YOUR STORY ON

Action is vital. It moves the story forward and, without it, you will not hold the reader's attention for long. Any part of a story or novel where characters are moving, talking or thinking can be called 'action'. So we have:

- Physical action
- Action through dialogue
- Mental action

Physical action

When we think of action we think of physical movement – someone chasing a thief down a road, a mother pushing a pram, a lorry driver on the motorway. In other words, someone doing something. And that is usually more exciting, more visual, than a static scene where, for instance, characters merely talk to each other.

Example:

Ella walked quickly down the pitch-black road. The ridiculous heels didn't help, nor the teeming rain. There being no one about just added to her nervousness. Crazy to be so scared … What was that? She stopped. Over the sound of the rain, footsteps, loud and clear – a man's footsteps. She hurried on, panic headlines going through her mind. 'Murder' … 'body found in road'. Now she was running … and the man behind her had also quickened his pace.

In such an active scene, the reader can really feel Ella's tension and fear as she hurries on. Physical action is a vivid, literal way of moving the story on.

Action through dialogue

Action can also take place in a static situation – through speech. Good dialogue is a great way of showing character. It can also be used as an effective way of moving the action forward, whilst also revealing new information. (See (15) 'Making Good Use of Dialogue')

Use physical action even while your characters are talking to each other. It helps to let one of them be DOING something, however insignificant. Such action adds to the scene and makes it far more visual.

Example:

'So, Ben, who are you going out with tonight?' Di asked, moving the iron over the shirt. She dreaded his answer.

'Sarah, actually. But what's it to you, Mum?' he added.

'What happened to Fiona?'

'No idea!'

Di took a deep breath, stabbing at the shirt collar. She hated collars. 'Chucked her, I suppose,' she said. 'Poor girl! Make ten of that Sarah.'

'Mum!'

A furious Ben rushed out of the room, slamming the door.

Di winced as she banged down the iron. She deserved that.

The conversation helps to develop the story and shows us the couple's reactions, so we also learn more about their characters.

Mental action

Sometimes you are restricted by the storyline and cannot use physical action or dialogue. Your viewpoint character might need to be alone to make an important decision that is vital to the situation. Then you'll need to get the action across through thoughts alone.

Example:

Angie found a seat on the crowded bus, vaguely aware of the babble of voices, the heat and the sweaty atmosphere. All she could think of was Sam and the pleading in his eyes as she walked away from him. She had done the right thing, of course. She shifted uncomfortably. Her future was the new job in America – new country, new people. Sam and this little market town would soon be part of her past. But she felt confused; excited and sad at the same time ...

That way of adding action can work very well. But remember that this is a passive way of using action (told through Angie's thoughts). Had the author used the discussion in an active way – that is, brought us in on the earlier scene when Angie and Sam are discussing the future (letting us actually hear them speak) – he would have been able to involve us more intimately with the couple. Showing the scene in a direct, physical way would have brought it to life. Because of the emotion and conflict involved in the situation, there is great opportunity for dramatic dialogue and physical action between Angie and Sam. What you have to ask yourself is whether or not that scene is crucial to the storyline. If you just wish to get Angie from A to B on the bus as quickly as possible, then the above example – written as 'mental action' – is fine.

Ideally, a short story or novel will include both physical and mental action, with some relevant direct dialogue. Some storylines demand a gentle approach, with hardly any physical action. Yet the story must still actively move on to its conclusion or the reader will get irritated or – worse – bored.

MASTERCLASS EXAMPLE

... Rapid steps thunder across the floor, there is a clattering across the ceiling, and dazzling beams of light sweep down the iron staircase and flood the cellar like high waves.

'Get down on the floor,' a man yells hysterically. 'Down on the floor!'

Simone is frozen to the spot.

'Lie down,' rasps Kennet.

'Shut your mouth!' someone yells.

'Down, down!'

Simone doesn't realize the men are talking to her until she feels a painful blow in the stomach that forces her to her knees.

(from *The Hypnotist* by Lars Kepler)

TOP TIP

If you have a very active scene, such as a chase, use short, staccato, sentences. They will give the effect of breathlessness and add to the atmosphere and tension.

USING ACTION TO MOVE YOUR STORY ON – THE MAIN POINTS

- Use direct action – unravelling the scene as it happens – wherever possible
- Using action along with dialogue makes the scene more visual
- A combination of physical and mental action – plus dialogue – is ideal

Exercise 1

Take one of the following situations and write it up as an action scene, using physical action, direct dialogue or thoughts – perhaps all three aspects. Use whichever form – or forms – of action you feel would suit the situation.

1. *A hold-up at a supermarket*
2. *A man packing his case, about to walk out on his girlfriend*
3. *A woman caught stealing cosmetics from a large store*

Exercise 2

Depict the following scene, using direct dialogue. Let the row build up to a crisis point and add the necessary action at the end.

   Two men are arguing in a pub. (Over a girl? You choose what the dispute is about!) *The argument gets nasty and ends up in a fight.*

(19)
SHOWING INSTEAD
OF TELLING

'Show, don't tell!' we are told. Most authors don't get this at first, so if you find it confusing, take heart. Keep writing and you will master it eventually; and understanding the concept will improve your writing style tremendously.

Telling

In the following scene, we need to get Fiona's personality and background across to the reader. We could do it this way:

Fiona was a headstrong girl of nineteen. She had always been a bit scatty and impulsive, liking to do her own thing. She longed to be independent and have her own flat. Her father ran his own computer business and could well afford to finance her, but refused. Her mother, too, thought Fiona was immature.

That paragraph holds all the information we want, but the author is telling us about it in a cold, formal way. The piece feels flat and uninviting.

Showing

Fiona tossed back her hair and glared defiantly at her father.

'All my mates have their own flats!' she cried. 'Why can't I?'

Dad just went on reading his paper and Fiona wanted to scream. Trapped, she was, in this dreary old house! No one had a clue how she felt. It was not as though he couldn't afford to buy her a flat. God, now Mum was about to chip in …

'We just don't think you're ready, Fiona,' she declared. 'You might be nineteen, but you're—' she hesitated.

'Irresponsible, stupid?' Fiona cried. 'At least I'm not as dull as you two!'

With that, she flounced out of the door.

There, the author:

- Has gone into Fiona's viewpoint to SHOW how she feels
- Has captured the scene mostly in dialogue, which brings out the other characters' feelings
- Does not need to TELL the reader anything. It is all SHOWN through dialogue and Fiona's thoughts.

The second version of the scene is far more interesting to read. Why? Because, by going into Fiona's viewpoint and using direct dialogue and thoughts, the author has drawn us in emotionally. And we must engage the reader emotionally or the story or novel will not work. There, we are into Fiona's viewpoint, so it is easier to show what is happening. The reader doesn't need to be told about events or feelings, because it is all shown through thoughts and dialogue.

There will be situations in short stories or novels where the only way you can get the information across is by 'telling'. Such as when:

- You have no characters 'on stage' and wish to describe something
- You are not into anyone's viewpoint
- You need to move quickly through an unimportant but necessary scene

A lot depends on the type of story or novel you are writing. Many classic books begin by *telling* the story – authors would begin their novels with atmospheric description and proceed to *tell* it. Then, later, they might go into a character's viewpoint and *show* the story, revealing feelings and emotion. Today, most readers prefer to identify with a character right from the start; they expect things to move a lot quicker. This is especially so in the short story where you are limited for words.

> **MASTERCLASS EXAMPLE**
> *(It is 1948. Hortense, just arrived in England from Jamaica, has a visit from her landlady)*
> ' ... Remember me? I let you in last night? Hortense, isn't it?'
> I did not wish to appear rude to this woman on my first day in England so I acknowledged her questions with a small nod of the head.
> 'Cat got your tongue?' she said. What cat was she talking of? Don't tell me there was a cat that must also live with us in this room. 'My name's Mrs Bligh,' she carried on. 'But you can call me Queenie, if you like. Everyone here does. Would you like that?' The impression I received was that she was talking to me as if I was an imbecile. An educated woman such as I.
> So I replied, 'Have you lost your cat?'
> And this woman's eyes rolled as if this was a question I had asked of her several times before.
>
> (from *Small Island* by Andrea Levy)

TOP TIP

The five senses – see, hear, taste, smell and touch – are significant when it comes to 'show, don't tell'. If, when they are taken into a café along with your character, your readers can smell the coffee as strongly as he can, you have mastered 'showing'.

SHOWING INSTEAD OF TELLING – THE MAIN POINTS
- In order to 'show', get right into the character's viewpoint
- Using dialogue and thoughts will help you to 'show', rather than 'tell'
- Merely telling your readers how someone feels will not engage them emotionally

Exercise 1

The following scene is 'told' to the reader. 'Show' it, by using direct dialogue, thoughts and emotions.

Pete ordered Danny to move three crates of veg from one market stall to the other. Danny got really angry with Pete. He was not the type to be bossed around in that manner and said so. He then told Pete where to stick his job.

Exercise 2
In a supermarket, Paula bumps into Anne, an old school pal she has not seen for years.

Keeping in Paula's viewpoint, show what she thinks of Anne, using dialogue and thoughts – but also by concentrating on one or both of these senses: sound and/or smell. Maybe Anne has a loud, shrieking voice or absolutely reeks of cheap perfume. Show how Paula reacts to it.

(20)
USING ALL FIVE SENSES TO IMPROVE YOUR WRITING

Sight, sound, taste, touch and smell. The five senses surround us all the time; we should be aware of them in our daily lives. But we tend to take them for granted. Authors often neglect to use them in their writing, forgetting how describing the taste of something, for example, can enrich a scene.

Sight

This is the prominent sense – perhaps the main one we take for granted. Most of us see a fictional scene in our minds before we begin to write about it. We visualise our characters – their appearance, emotions and expressions – imagining every movement and mood they are about to go through. Then we proceed to put that on paper. And it is fair to say that most authors make a pretty good job of transferring their visual images.

But even this most familiar of senses needs thinking about. Is that scene or person coming across a bit clichéd? And it might be worth taking another look at the way you've described the landscape. Has it been done before like that? Can you find a fresh way of writing about those sweeping green fields? We often need to look again; try to see the scene or character from a different perspective. Not easy – and it will take extra time. But any fresh view is bound to improve the quality of the writing.

The simplest detail can be overlooked. Take colour, for instance. It can bring your story to life.

Example:

He stood gazing after her as she merged into the pavement crowds and vanished from sight, out of his life. Then he shrugged and walked on.

Now add some colour:

He stood gazing after her, clinging to the sight of her bright red jacket till it merged into the pavement crowds and she vanished from sight, out of his life. Then he shrugged and walked on.

The second version might be slightly longer, but that little bit of colour adds so much to the scene.

Sound

This sense can be used to good effect. But, again, try to find a new – sometimes more accurate – way of describing sound. Listen more closely to familiar noises. Does a cat's protest, for instance, really come over as 'meow'? Often it is more a 'ye-o-o-wl'! (James Joyce, apparently, wrote 'mrkneow' for 'meow'!) Does a clock really tick-tock? Does a duck quack or a kettle hum?

As with sight, it is easier – and tempting – to use clichés. But it pays to spend a little more time and come up with something fresh. And don't be afraid to convey silences and pauses – vital to the playwright and very effective and atmospheric in any fiction writing.

Taste

Often neglected, this sense can, literally, add flavour to your writing! Suppose, in a story or novel, a man and a girl are sitting in a restaurant. They have met to talk about splitting up and the author, quite rightly, is intent on writing an emotional scene in order to get the problem across; the outcome is crucial. The setting being a restaurant, there is opportunity to add the sense of taste (and smell). Yet often, in restaurant scenes, the food itself is overlooked by the writer. You might get clichéd expressions, such as 'he drained his wine glass', or 'she merely toyed with her food', but the meal itself is hardly mentioned.

Example:

Stuart began to eat. He was ravenous and the food tasted really delicious. He felt guilty, having booked this meal to tell Della he was leaving her.

'You're not eating anything, darling,' he said.

Or:

Stuart began to eat. He was ravenous; beef – medium rare in a thick, rich gravy – just the way he liked it. He felt guilty, having booked this meal to tell Della he was leaving her.

'You're not eating anything, darling,' he said.

Touch

This is another, often neglected, sense which can add so much to the quality of your writing. Touch the desk or table around your keyboard. What does it feel like? Hard, solid, smooth, rough, pitted? Close your eyes and pick up a familiar object, such as a ring, without looking at it. How does it feel? Round, of course, but what else? Is there engraving on it, are the stones rough-edged, is it as smooth as you would have believed?

When you are writing, you probably won't need to describe things in such detail but getting a new perspective on them will help. Try making a conscious effort to concentrate on things you usually take for granted. Pets, for instance; we usually stroke a cat or dog without thinking about it. Try thinking about it. How does the coat feel? Silky, rough, warm? Tangled, murky, coarse?

Touch, in fiction, is important. It is all about communication – and where would the human race be without that? Whatever form of fiction you are working on – and not just in the romantic genre – try to add touch. Human beings need to connect. Handshakes, for instance, can help to depict character. You might say that a half-hearted handshake shows a weak person and a vice-like grip a more powerful one. Or is that idea a bit clichéd? (You could always give the weak character the strong handshake and vice versa!) Whatever, you will have introduced touch.

Other 'touch' clichés are: a soft pillow, a plastic credit card, a hard pavement, a wobbly jelly and so on. Try to find fresh ways of describing them. (See (26) 'Making Vital Contact Between Characters')

Smell

What can you smell at the moment? Believe it or not, there is usually a smell within close proximity, wherever you are. An empty room will smell of dust, damp, staleness. You will be surrounded by an aroma or atmosphere, even if you can't put a name to it. Smell is often the first thing you encounter going into a strange building. If at all possible, bring this sense into your writing – it will add so much to the atmosphere.

It has been said that humans see the world, but most animals smell it. Think about cats and dogs – they will always sniff first. Smell, of all the senses, is said to be the most evocative – the one that brings back the past, for instance, most vividly. Smelling something that you've not smelled for years can bring back long forgotten memories of people, things and places. A new perfume might remind you of one you used in your teens; a smell of baking might help you recall your childhood.

How do you describe this sense to readers? Of all the five, the sense of smell has to be the most difficult. Bad, rotten, sweet, sharp, sickly are all a bit clichéd. Experience the smell once more, if possible, then try to come up with an original description. Not easy!

MASTERCLASS EXAMPLE

It wasn't only being alone; it was the way the house smelt dead.

She sat under a big sweet-chestnut tree, in the heart of the woodland, watching Mr Thompson with grave brown eyes. Mr Thompson was frying mushrooms over a hazel fire in an old half-circular billy-can. The peculiar aroma of hazel smoke and the tang of mushrooms was so strong on the October evening air that every now and then she licked her lips like someone in a hungry dream.

'Never had wild mushrooms before,' she said. 'Never knew you could get them wild.'

(the beginning of 'And No Birds Sing', a short story by H. E. Bates)

TOP TIP

Examine closely the everyday things around you, listen intently to sound, including voices. Think about how your food tastes – really tastes. Examine how an object feels in detail. Observe smells wherever you are. *Write it all down!*

USING ALL FIVE SENSES TO IMPROVE YOUR WRITING – THE MAIN POINTS

- Sight and sound will usually be prominent in your writing. Don't neglect the other three senses
- Add the senses at any opportunity
- Look for a fresh way of describing each of them

Exercise 1

Describe some – or all – of the following things or situations in as few words as possible. Try to think of an original way of doing so.

- *The taste of a strawberry*
- *The smell of an indoor swimming pool*
- *The touch of an inflated balloon*
- *The sound of tyres over snow*
- *The smell of onions frying*
- *The taste of cheese*
- *The smell of a hospital ward*
- *The touch of a baby's fingers*
- *The sound of ducks at the water's edge*
- *The taste of chocolate*

Exercise 2

In a notebook, write the headings: SIGHT, SOUND, TASTE, TOUCH, SMELL; taking one page for each subject. Take the notebook with you to your next assignment or appointment, be it dentist, doctor, supermarket, park or whatever. Consciously think about what your senses are experiencing and write down your observations.

(21)
BRINGING ABOUT CHANGE

A good place to start a short story or novel is at the point of change; when something new – preferably a move which heralds conflict – is about to happen in someone's life. It doesn't always have to be a big action change, such as moving house, a new job, divorce or a death in the family. Often a main character will have come to an emotional decision or have changed his outlook on something important. That type of change can be just as traumatic and lead on to an intriguing story. Whatever, you need something to pull the reader in – and a point of change provides a really good hook.

Character change
Many authors appear to do the opposite of what we've all been taught, yet produce works of genius! But there is one guideline with which it pays to comply – your main character needs to have changed in some way by the end of the story or novel. Let's suppose you've started the story at a point of physical change. Maybe your main character needs to move with his job and he and the family are reluctant to go. By the end of the story, after going through the traumas, joys and experiences of their new life, they will probably have changed their opinions and also their outlook.

There are many ways your main character can change. Emotionally, for instance, he could go through a bitter experience and emerge from that with a totally different slant on life. Or life could deal him a physical blow – an illness or bad accident. Perhaps, at the start of the story, he is a weak character with a shocking past history and, through his own mistakes, learns a valuable lesson by the end. Whatever, if he has stayed as he was at the beginning – learned nothing through his experiences – what is the point of the story?

Try not to spell out any changes in an obvious way. You should not need to – your character's experiences will have sign-posted them and the reader should pick them up. A change in characterisation is always better when done subtly. Readers can then work out for themselves that the person they have laughed and cried with all the way through has changed (usually) for the better. But remember that the change must come about because of what happens in the story – not through some sudden revelation!

Example:

Dave spends every Saturday at football, leaving his wife to cope with two young children. The wife is very unhappy about this and confides in her friend. The friend tries to tell Dave, who is furious at what he calls interference [which adds another complication and holds up the ending]. *One Saturday, one of the children is involved in an accident and the wife cannot contact Dave. The upshot is that when he finally gets to the hospital Dave realises how selfish he's been and agrees to curb some of his beloved matches.*

Now, that might appear to be a rather weak plot, but it serves a purpose. Through what happens in the story the problem is solved: Dave has 'learned his lesson', if you like. And – importantly – *changed*.

Loopholes NOT to be used when effecting character change. Never:

- Allow another character to merely talk him into changing
- Allow him to wake up one morning and 'see the light'
- Allow him to suddenly change character for no reason. People don't

If, when you get to the revision stage, you realise that your character is thinking and acting in exactly the same way as he was at the beginning, ask yourself whether the story works. You could, of course, be aiming to show what happens if someone refuses to change. An example is the prizewinning novel *The Remains of the*

Day, by Kazuo Ishiguro. Stevens (the narrator and main character, a butler in a big house) tells the story of his working and personal life, including the upheavals brought by World War II, throughout which he stubbornly refuses to change. And, by the end, the storyline becomes a tragedy to us, the readers ... yet not really for Stevens.

Maybe, in your novel, the change has happened to a minor character. If so, has it had an effect on your main character who, after all, is the person your reader will identify with? If not, think again. Maybe, for the story to work, you need a rewrite, making your minor character the main viewpoint person?

MASTERCLASS EXAMPLE
(Young Laura has just seen her first dead body, that of a young man. Afterwards, she meets her brother, Laurie)

'I say, you're not crying, are you?' asked her brother.

Laura shook her head. She was.

Laurie put his arm round her shoulder. 'Don't cry,' he said in his warm, loving voice. 'Was it awful?'

'No,' sobbed Laura. 'It was simply marvellous. But, Laurie—' She stopped, she looked at her brother. 'Isn't life,' she stammered, 'isn't life—' But what life was she couldn't explain. No matter. He quite understood.

'*Isn't* it, darling?' said Laurie.

(the ending of 'The Garden Party', a short story by Katherine Mansfield)

TOP TIP

Remember that any change in character – especially if it is quite major – must be believable. Remind yourself how you painted the character at the start and ask yourself whether the storyline would really have affected him in that way.

BRINGING ABOUT CHANGE – THE MAIN POINTS
• Your main character should have changed in some way by the end of the story

- The change must come about because of what happened in the story
- A subtle change – between the lines, so to speak – works well

Exercise 1

Work out a plot involving change for one or more of the following characters:

- *A shy accountant, who fancies a colleague but daren't ask her out*
- *A bossy shop manager who tends to bully her staff*
- *A lonely pensioner who rebuffs anyone who tries to befriend her*

Exercise 2

What action could have led up to the following ending of a short story? Something that happened earlier in the story has changed Marie's attitude to dogs. Write up a possible plot.

Marie stooped down to stroke Jasper. She smiled to herself, feeling great. A couple of days ago she could never have done that ...

(22)
MANAGING STRUCTURE

Structure – how the story is arranged to give the best effect – is of great importance. It is how you put together the emotional, dramatic, action-packed or static scenes in order to make the most impact. As previously stated in (9) 'Deciding Whether or Not to Plan', structure is intertwined with planning and plotting; the structure is the putting together of the story to give the best result. You may need to show irony, arrange the story to create extra suspense or decide that a twist ending would add zest to the story. That is giving it good structure.

The short story
Short story writers should examine published authors' work from their chosen market. How much action, direct dialogue, thoughts and reactions will you need in order to sell to that particular magazine? How is each aspect positioned – does the magazine prefer you to open with dialogue, for instance? The short story writer's approach to structure must be different from the novelist's. The over-all impression has to be what Edgar Allan Poe called 'the single effect'. A short story must make a single emotional impact and reach a conclusion in a sharp economic way, whilst a novel, with time and length on its side, can raise many questions and complex issues.

The novel
In the same way, novelists should study published authors from their chosen genre. That way you will see roughly how many scenes and chapters you are likely to need – how their length, the action,

dramatic events, dialogue and quieter scenes balance out. In other words, you will see how the novel is structured. If you are worried about the length of scenes and chapters – whether you have enough material or too much, how many characters you'll need to tell your story, how much flashback – begin with some kind of plan. You might not be a natural planner, but try to see it this way: would anyone go off on an adventure to unknown territory without a map, or start building a house without a plan? At the very least, rough planning will give you the confidence to start. (See (9) 'Deciding Whether or Not to Plan')

Remember that, when you are constructing your plot, you'll need to contrast scenes. If you have loads of breathless adventure and drama planned for a couple of chapters you may then want to slow things down with a quieter emotional or reflective chapter or scene, to allow readers to catch their breath. Or you could move on to a sub-plot. You will be able to judge the pace of the book better when you do an over-all read through at the end.

MASTERCLASS EXAMPLE

Structure is what assembles the parts of a story in a way that makes them accessible to readers. It is the orderly arrangement of story material for the benefit of the audience. Structure is about timing – where in the mix those elements go.

(from *Plot & Structure* by James Scott Bell)

TOP TIP

Give some thought to the time element of your story or novel. If it is an action story it is better taking place over a shorter period of time. A longer time span will suit the structure of a slower-paced story.

MANAGING STRUCTURE – THE MAIN POINTS
- Do a rough plan before you start
- Check that your scenes are balanced. Is any part of the story too rushed or too drawn-out?

• To understand structure, read and study the work of other authors

Exercise 1

Write a short, short story of around 500 words using the following idea. Choose whose viewpoint you tell the story from (the father, mistress, daughter or boyfriend). Structure the story so that all the very brief scenes are balanced and lead up to a gripping climax. Create a single emotional impact leaving the reader with one over-all feeling: amusement, irony or whatever.

Unbeknown to his family, a married man is having an affair. He takes his mistress to a restaurant. Unexpectedly, his daughter arrives for a meal with her boyfriend.

Exercise 2

Now rewrite the story, using the same idea but starting at a different time and place. If you begin it earlier, before the restaurant scene, how will you 'grab' the reader? Give the story a different structure by incorporating a surprise ending.

(23)
USING FLASHBACK

Ideally, all fiction should be what is happening *now*. Flashback – where characters think back to the past to show how they came to be in the predicament they are in – can hold up the story. That applies to both the short story and the novel. In a short story the flashbacks – if any – must be few and really brief. And even in the longer novel, readers will still be impatient to get back to the main storyline to learn how things turn out. Long flashbacks rarely work. Yet a certain amount of flashback is usually necessary, especially at the beginning of a story.

Example:

'Just Hair' was busy, but Blanche hardly noticed.

'Have you planned a holiday this year?' smiled Lynn.

Through the mirror, Blanche stared blankly at the stylist, who was trying to do something with her thinning hair. Holiday – some hopes! After Rod's shocking announcement at breakfast …

'Got something to tell you, Blanche,' he'd said.

She had scarcely heard him over baby William's shrieks, but then he told her to sit down.

'Planned a holiday, Mrs Jenkins?' Lynn repeated.

Startled, Blanche came back to the present.

'No.' She made an effort. 'What about you?'

Allowing the girl to prattle on about Majorca and boyfriends, Blanche's thoughts took a much uglier path … back to the scene at breakfast.

' … Tracy and I … we're in love,' Rod said. 'I'm so sorry!'

At first, she'd just gone on calmly shovelling cereal into William. Then she let rip.

'You're sorry?' she sneered.

In that scene, flashback is used to get information over to the reader. You allow the character to think back – usually when she is doing something else. You can then interrupt the thinking back with what is happening now, as in the above example – reminding the reader of the main story. But don't recount too much flashback.

For instance, you might be tempted to add more of Blanche's reaction at breakfast time, or tell how Rod stormed out of the house. Don't! We now know what her problem is and that is all we need at present. Any other clues as to why the marriage is not working can be threaded in throughout the story. You must now concentrate on how Blanche will cope and what she will do about the situation when she leaves the hairdresser's – the main action.

Avoiding flashback

Sometimes it is possible to avoid going back in time altogether. In that hairdressing scene, for example, you could have Blanche telling Lynn what happened, perhaps have her dissolving in tears. Maybe Lynn and Blanche are good friends and Lynn is about to play a prominent part in the story. In that case it would be appropriate for Blanche to reveal all to Lynn.

Another way is to start the story earlier. Ask yourself: are my flashback scenes more dramatic or significant than what happens later? If they appear to be, perhaps you should have used them as though they are happening now? Take our example – had you started it at the breakfast table you would not need flashback. The entire scene could have been played out there and then. You might still need to convey more information, of course – maybe we need to know how he met the new girlfriend, or about some hitch in the marriage. That could be done through Blanche's thoughts later. But it is important to keep flashback to a minimum or you risk boring your reader by holding up the story. You want just enough to make the situation clear.

Cliff-hanger flashback

Try, if you possibly can, to put your main character in an intriguing situation before you go into flashback. That way you will promise the reader something interesting to go back to after the interruption of the flashback. A rather clichéd example would be if your character was a passenger on a plane that had engine problems. In that situation, after the initial panic, it would be quite natural for the person to reminisce about his life. You could have him reveal something in his past which was relevant to the story. Even if that went on a bit you would hopefully still keep your reader's interest because of what is to come later. Will the plane crash?

Natural flashback

If it is necessary to use flashback, make it natural. Put it in when the person would normally have time to think back or reminisce: in the dentist's waiting room, during a sleepless night or perhaps during a train journey. A young mother hurrying to cope with a screaming baby is unlikely to think back wistfully to her teenage years at that point, or only very briefly. Longer flashback would be more natural when the baby is asleep!

Hads

An odd subtitle, but a significant one. Grammatically, when you use flashback you automatically go into the past perfect tense: *He had done this, he had decided that* ... You are telling of something that happened before, so you correctly use 'had' to recall incidents, dialogue and scenes that the reader needs to know. But, stick strictly to that 'rule' and you end up with the following:

As she waited for her brother's train to arrive, Stella thought back to the last time she had seen Terry. Twenty years ago ...

He had been about eighteen, tall and fair, and he had always had a ready smile. She had been about twelve, if that. They had gone to the park with his pal.

'Gonna get some ices, Stella,' Terry had said. 'Be back soon!'

She had hung about for ages. But she never saw him or his pal again.

Now, on this draughty station, she felt anxious. Supposing she didn't recognise Terry?

You have to use 'had' because Stella is thinking back to when it *had* happened. But, rather than pepper the page with 'hads' which, after a while, can really grate, it reads better if you just use the first one or two – to denote that you've gone back in time – and then drop them.

Proceed as though you are writing in the present; as though it were the main story (though, of course, it is not). Doing it this way makes it more immediate for the reader and you get rid of the dreaded 'hads'. So long as you make it absolutely clear when you go into flashback, then again when you come out of it, it will work.

Example:

As she waited for her brother's train to arrive, Stella thought back to the last time she had seen Terry. Twenty years ago …

He had been about eighteen, tall and fair and with a ready smile. She was about twelve, if that. They were in the park with his pal.

'Gonna get some ices, Stella,' Terry said. 'Be back soon!'

She hung about for ages. But she never saw him or his pal again.

Now, on this draughty station, she felt anxious. Supposing she didn't recognise Terry?

Back story

There will be times when you need to explain vital back story to the reader from an omniscient viewpoint – that is, when you cannot do it from inside the mind of a character and you are writing in a detached way (see (13) 'Understanding Omniscient Viewpoint').

Example:

The crowd pressed forward. One of the men, Gerald Grant, was waving a huge stick and could have killed anyone with it. It was well known that Gerald had been abused as a child. His family were all thugs – his father and brother had been in prison for years.

Again, keep back story as brief as possible and move on with the main story.

MASTERCLASS EXAMPLE

(Minas Nolan lives with Tommy's mother, Branwyn, and has brought Tommy up. He is telling the boy that he now has to go to live with his real father)

'... He *(a lawyer)* told me that because your mother and I never married that Madeline and your father have legal guardianship.'

'But why didn't you get married?'

'I asked her, Tommy, I asked her every month. But she always said no.'

Thomas thought about the lunch he had with his mother and father. Elton *(his father)* had kissed Branwyn on the mouth before they left. At first she seemed to be kissing him back, but then she pushed him away and after that she spent the day crying.

Looking up into Minas Nolan's sad face, Thomas knew somehow that he was the reason they could not marry.

(from *Fortunate Son* by Walter Mosley)

TOP TIP

Once you are in flashback, try to put as much information as possible into direct dialogue. This makes it more immediate and readable.

USING FLASHBACK – THE MAIN POINTS

- Keep it brief. Readers are more interested in how the main story develops
- Make it immediate. After one or two 'hads', write it as though it is happening now
- Be absolutely clear that you are now going back in time. And be just as clear when you get back to the main story

Exercise 1

A plot centres round a teenage boy's love of motorcycle racing. The father does not approve because he is in a wheelchair – the result of an accident he himself had whilst participating in the sport.

Using flashback, write a scene from the father's point of view, showing how he feels as he thinks back to the time of the accident. Then bring the reader back to the present. The story is to be only 800 words, so the flashback must be extremely brief.

Exercise 2

Cut as many 'hads' as possible:

She remembered when she had first met him.

'What job do you do?' she had asked him. She had not liked to pry, but she had felt she needed to know.

'Bus driver,' he had replied. Then he had gone on to tell her lots of things that had happened on his bus.

'Sounds interesting!' she had laughed, wondering how much of it was true.

Meeting him again now, he seemed completely different.

(24)
STRENGTHENING
THE MIDDLE

The middle of a short story or novel can be a bit of a danger zone. The author, having had a brilliant idea, will start easily enough and plunge excitedly into the beginning. Chances are that he has a vague idea of the ending, too. And the middle? Often that is left to take care of itself: 'Oh, that will come as I write,' he says. Great … if it does. But supposing the idea peters out? The danger is that the whole story might collapse at that point.

You start off well and then realise that the story will not logically work. The original idea does not seem so brilliant after all. A vague plan might have kept you going, but who knows? If you are one of those authors with masses of ideas, you just start another story or novel. Whether you get past the middle next time is anyone's guess! A pity, when you've already put so much work into this idea …

What is the middle?
The middle is the main body of the story, showing a series of scenes and interchanges in which the main character (or characters) tries to solve the problem which was presented in the opening scenes. The key thing to think about when writing the middle – and indeed, all the way through the story – is *suspense*. You must keep the suspense going, adding more and more obstacles (depending on the length), building tension all the time, until the climax. Every scene, event or piece of dialogue must add to the suspense, making it more and more impossible for that initial problem to be solved. How on earth will he or she find a satisfactory solution? This is the question that keeps readers reading.

Lack of suspense is usually to blame for the 'sagging' which occurs all too often in the middle section. The book or short story often dips at that point. Sometimes it is because the plot is not strong enough to sustain the length, or the story has become so confusing that all suspense is weakened.

The secret of the middle of the story is to keep things moving – dramatically, emotionally or whatever – towards the climax. Yet, at the same time, you must hold your reader back from the outcome.

There are several things to avoid:

A weak plot

Your story needs to be strong enough to keep people reading. 'Strong', in that sense, does not necessarily mean epic events and powerful characters. You can write a light story with hardly any action, yet give the plot a strong emotional element and tension, which builds up to the end. A weak plot is more likely to be one with no movement, either dramatically or emotionally, and where the characters do not change at all.

Predictability

Once your story becomes predictable you might as well give up. If, in the middle, you signal the ending and the outcome is obvious, why would readers carry on reading?

Short story plot example:

Beginning: *A girl is obsessed with a lad who, unbeknown to her, is always in trouble.*

Middle: *A 'good' guy, who likes her, appears on the scene. She is not really interested in him. The first lad involves her in some illegal set-up and things go from bad to worse.*

Ending: *The good guy comes to her rescue – she is now interested. And it all ends happily ever after …*

A clichéd plot, but it demonstrates predictability. From the minute the good guy appears, we can predict the ending. It is obvious that he is put in for a reason. An even worse fault is when a reader can guess the end right from the beginning. Why bother to read on? Predictability, usually introduced in the middle of the story, is one of the main reasons for rejection by editors.

Plot confusion

It is so easy, especially in the middle of your story, to confuse the reader. Have you tried to get in too much action and information – is it all too hurried? If it is a novel, maybe you could withhold some of the information till later, giving the reader even more incentive to read on. Or is it all too drawn out and therefore boring? Read through the middle again. Is it balanced, compared with the rest of the novel? If your short story is confusing, perhaps you have introduced too many characters?

Keeping the initial problem central

Have you kept the initial problem central to your story all the way through? In a novel, you may also have a sub-plot, but the central storyline is crucial. If the main story is Darryl's, you might feel it is necessary to reveal his teenage nephew's dubious exploits. Showing Darryl's opinion of the lad will bring out more of Darryl's character. Great – but don't go into the exploits in too great a depth. Unless, of course, they are really important to Darryl's story.

Dramatising the wrong scenes

You, the author, have to decide which scenes to expand upon and which to skip over. This will depend on the story. Whose story is it? If an upcoming scene involves that person and will affect the outcome of the story, then you will need to dramatise it. OK, that sounds like stating the obvious, but it is easy to exaggerate the wrong scenes. A car journey could be dismissed in a line: *It took him just ten minutes to get to the club.* Unless, of course, you want the reader to know what is going on in his mind while he is driving. Then you might linger longer on the car ride. Ask yourself: do I need that scene? If you are increasing the tension and adding to the story, then you probably do.

> **MASTERCLASS EXAMPLE**
> ... The middle is a bridge ... Unity in fiction depends on keeping everybody on the bridge. The forces developed in the middle must emerge naturally out of the characters and situation introduced at the beginning. In turn, the ending must make use of those same forces and conflicts, with nothing important left out and nothing new suddenly appearing at the last minute. The middle develops the implicit promise by 'dramatizing incidents'.
>
> (from *Beginnings, Middles & Ends* by Nancy Kress)

TOP TIP

Keep any unfinished manuscripts that 'died' halfway through. After a gap in time, look at them again. You may see a way you can get through what Philip Larkin called the 'muddle of the middle'.

STRENGTHENING THE MIDDLE – THE MAIN POINTS
• Keep it clear
• Keep your main character's problem at the forefront of the story. Then add to the problem to make it worse
• Keep building the suspense. No sagging in the middle!

Exercise 1

Select and read a short story from a magazine, or root out a favourite novel. Where would you say the middle began and ended? Is it balanced with the rest of the story? Study it carefully and be as critical as you like. Would you have written the middle differently?

Exercise 2

This shows the beginning and ending of a short story plot. The story is to be around 1,000 words in length, told from the mother's viewpoint.

You fill in the middle.

Beginning: *The story opens with the mother trying to stop her son from joining the Army. There is a terrible row and the son walks out.*

Middle:

Ending: *Because of what happens in the middle of the story, she comes to terms with him going.*

(25)
CREATING A
SATISFACTORY ENDING

A satisfactory ending comes about when the author finally solves
the problems, and answers the questions which are presented at the
beginning. The middle of the story will have dramatised situations
– adding even more obstacles and complications – and the ending
supplies the solution.

Endings must:

- Satisfy
- Be logical
- Deliver emotion
- Never cheat the reader
- Have, if possible, an element of surprise

Above all, an ending must follow through from what was promised
at the opening. As the story moves forward, the solution must grow
naturally out of the action and the characters' personalities. Only
then will it satisfy the reader. The ending does not necessarily have to
be happy, but it must be logical. In other words, it needs to come
over as credible and suit the tone of the story.

Emotion is the main reason people read fiction – they need to feel
something as they finish reading. You aim to have aroused emotion –
love, rage, sympathy, or whatever. Never cheat the reader at the end:
don't be tempted to solve a complex problem the easy way, perhaps by
conveniently bringing in a new character or a situation foreign to the
preceding plot. Coincidence, too, is taboo. Years ago, authors might
have got away with using it to tie up a story, but not today.

The short story
If you are writing a commercial short story – one that you hope to

sell to a magazine or perhaps online – market study is paramount. The approach to the ending has to be different than that for the 'literary' story, or one aimed at a competition, where you might still have to watch length, etc., or use a set theme, but would be less restricted.

As mentioned elsewhere in this book, for those hoping to sell their work, the traditional women's magazines are the main short story markets today. And their editors have always preferred what they call 'an upbeat' ending – they don't like to leave their readers feeling down. Now, that does not necessarily mean a soppy, 'happy ever after' finish. If a rather sad, reflective ending is more logical for your particular story, that's fine. But you are more likely to sell it if you can insert what magazines call 'a note of hope' somewhere.

For instance, let's say that at the end of your story you have your heroine realise that Dean is not the guy for her and the story finishes with her all alone. Another guy hovering in the background might help you to sell it. While the trauma with Dean is going on, you could mention 'Tom' at some point. Perhaps she likes Tom but never took him that seriously. She and Tom might not be 'an item' at the end, but maybe in the future … There you have your note of hope! Or you could make her a really independent character, so that in the back of her mind she is quite relieved to be free of Dean and the reader knows she will be fine on her own. You need some reassurance, just so that readers can feel 'upbeat' about the ending. (Preferring sad endings, I lost count of the rejection slips I stacked up at first!)

Never rush the final scenes. Sometimes, with a short story, you can almost feel the author's relief to get it finished because the ending seems to be hurried or just tacked on. At the other end of the scale, make sure all loose ends are tied up, but don't go rambling on after the natural end is reached. The end must balance with the rest of the story and, above all, it must make readers have some kind of emotional reaction. Have they learned something? Perhaps a character or his actions impressed them. They need to feel differently through having read the story.

Ask yourself: has my main character changed? (See (21) 'Bringing About Change') And try to bring in an element of surprise at the end. Something unexpected, however small, will add so much to the plot.

Twist-ending short stories

These are usually very short – 1,000 words or under – and popular in today's magazines. Basically, the author 'hoodwinks' the reader into thinking that the story and its characters are going in one direction. At the end, the story is 'turned on its head' – the reader is surprised to find things are not at all as they seemed. The twist usually involves the main character – he often turns out not to be the person the reader thinks he is. But do keep him human – having him turn out to be a monkey or cat or whatever, at the end, is taboo! You need a certain type of skill – and an original idea – to carry off this type of story. Because the ending has to be a complete surprise to the reader, such a story needs to be plotted first.

Example:

Your viewpoint character is preparing for a wedding later that day, looking at her dress, doing her hair, etc. But she has doubts about getting married. The reader is led to think the doubts are the usual last-minute panic. She chats to her bridesmaid, who tries to reassure her.

After more agonising, she turns up at the church, sees her bridegroom and everything is OK. In the last line you reveal that she is no young, innocent girl but a woman of 68. The bridesmaid is her granddaughter. Her doubts had been about getting married again so late in life.

You would write that story as though from a young bride's angle, now and again putting in a tiny clue (very tiny, or you'll give it away) as to the actual circumstances. Editors like clues, so that readers looking back can think: 'Oh, of course – I should have guessed at that point!' The main 'rule' here is to keep the secret until at least the last paragraph. Better still, the last sentence ... or even better, the last word:

Jane walked up the aisle towards the smiling grey-haired man waiting for her. She grinned as she handed her bouquet to her granddaughter. Age was only a number. She felt 28, not 68.

The novel

The ending of a novel is crucial in that it must satisfy and give a logical conclusion. Whether or not you finish on a happy-ever-after note will depend on the genre and tone of the story. You have a freer hand here and are not so tied to market requirements, but if you choose to leave the end 'open', thereby leaving much to the reader's imagination and intelligence, make sure you've got it right. In general, people are not keen on having to work out for themselves what might have happened to the characters. You are the writer and they expect you to wrap up the story. The reader has stuck with you throughout 80,000 words or so and will be sorely disappointed to be let down at the end, especially if they feel they deserved more of a 'rounding up'.

Some questions to think about:

- Have you tied up all necessary loose ends?
- What about the sub-plot? In your eagerness to resolve the main story have you given enough time and thought to your secondary storyline and its characters?
- Have you checked on all the characters? What about poor Auntie Flo, mentioned in Chapter Four and never heard of again? Did you need her at all?
- Have your characters got what they deserved?
- Have you fulfilled the promises you made in the opening chapters?
- Is the ending rushed? Does it balance out with the rest of the story?

- Has the ending gone on … and on? Could the story have finished earlier?
- Is the ending logical? (No cheating the reader with coincidences; no sudden appearance of new characters in order conveniently to tie things up)
- Is there an element of surprise somewhere?
- Is the ending clear?

MASTERCLASS EXAMPLE

… The stars still twinkled intensely. He was too spent to think of anything to say; she was too overcome with grief and fear and a little resentment. He looked down at the pale blotch of her face upturned from the low meadow beyond the fence. The thorn boughs tangled above her, drooping behind her like the roof of a hut. Beyond was the great width of the darkness. He felt unable to gather his energy to say anything vital.

'Goodbye,' he said. 'I'm going back – on Saturday. But – you'll write to me. Goodbye.'

He turned to go. He saw her white uplifted face vanish, and her dark form bend under the boughs of the tree, and go out into the great darkness. She did not say goodbye.

(the ending of 'A Modern Lover', a short story by D. H. Lawrence)

TOP TIP

If you have written a twist-ending story, read it through twice to check it works both ways. First, read it the 'wrong' way – the story you want the reader to believe. Then check that it works from the second, correct angle. In the given example, you would first read that story as though the viewpoint character is a young bride. Then reread it, this time from an older woman's viewpoint.

CREATING A SATISFACTORY ENDING – THE MAIN POINTS
- Is it clear?
- It must be logical and provide a solution, leading on from the situation presented at the opening

• It must not go on after the major problem is solved

Exercise 1
Look again at the last paragraph of your favourite novels or a published short story. Did you find the end satisfactory? Try rewriting the final paragraph to see if you think you could improve on it.

Exercise 2
Short story plot:

A woman has searched to find her son. He was adopted eighteen years ago. She has been through all the proper channels, the Internet, etc. and is at last to come face to face with him. They meet in a café. Is he pleased, angry or disinterested on meeting his mother?

Write the final scene of the story in full, in around 300 words.

SECTION THREE:
BLENDING ESSENTIAL INGREDIENTS

(26)
MAKING VITAL CONTACT BETWEEN CHARACTERS

Contact between your main characters is essential in a commercial short story. If you are writing a story about relationships, you need to get the pair together in some way – through dialogue, action, reaction, flashback or whatever. And physical contact between them is even better. Readers want to see them together, even if they hate each other! In the novel, with its longer time span and room for development of character, this lack of contact between main characters is not so likely. But contact is important; we tend to assume that the main characters, being crucial to the story, are bound to meet at some stage.

Yet it is easy to write a short story with no actual contact between the characters. In one of my early stories I had my viewpoint character dreamily thinking of her ex-boyfriend; how wonderful he was, the rows they'd had, how they'd split up. I kept it all in her mind, telling her story to the reader. The manuscript came back with a rejection letter, commenting: *boyfriend much too shadowy.* Shadowy was an understatement, because the poor man never actually appeared in the story! What I should have done was to use flashback scenes in an immediate sense – as though they were happening now – so that the two people came alive on the page. (See (23) 'Using Flashback'.)

An example of how I did it (the wrong way):

Debbie sipped her coffee. The man on the next table, sitting with his girlfriend, looked a bit like Jake, with the same dark untidy hair. She and Jake had sat like that, holding hands, the day he told her how much he loved her. He had said it so tenderly that she foolishly believed him. Now she felt angry with herself …

The following example is better, bringing in the flashback as though it's happening now and therefore bringing the pair together:

Debbie stared at the couple on the next table. The man, tall and dark, looked a bit like her Jake. She thought back to that memorable day in another restaurant ...

'Debs, I really love you, you know,' Jake had said gruffly, touching her hand across the table.

She'd felt as though she were in a dream. Was this really happening to her? She smiled at Jake. There was real tenderness in his eyes and her hand felt warm and safe under his.

'I love you, too, Jake,' she said.

Debbie sighed now. Sitting here alone, that day seemed unreal ...

In the second example, the 'absent' character is brought to life. We actually see and hear Jake in that scene – he is no longer shadowy. By showing what happened between the characters, instead of merely telling the story, the reader is brought closer to Jake, providing the vital contact. And, for good measure, there is also physical contact between the characters.

MASTERCLASS EXAMPLE

(Deborah is having her portrait painted by Leigh)

'... D'you mind?' He put his hand on my head and began to fiddle with the comb.

I hadn't realised how intimate the painting of a portrait can become. He used any excuse, putting his fingers on my neck to turn my head, grasping my shoulders with warm hands, smoothing the dress round my hips. It was a sort of mock love-making in a Laurence Sterne way, and I cursed myself for being such a fool. But I didn't all that much want it to stop. That was really the awful thing.

(from *The Walking Stick* by Winston Graham)

TOP TIP

Use the sense of touch wherever you can. Merely brushing against someone's sleeve can provide emotional contact and help bring a character alive.

MAKING VITAL CONTACT BETWEEN CHARACTERS – THE MAIN POINTS

- Always make sure you bring your main characters together in some way
- If an important character cannot be present in the story, bring him to life through flashback
- Physical contact will aid characterisation

Exercise 1

Concentrating on contact between characters, write a scene from the following plot.

Jason is unhappily married and wants to get in touch with Fiona, a girl he knew years ago. He becomes obsessed by thoughts of her and thinks back to the old days. He knew her when he was in his twenties, when he had ambitions to become a stage magician. He tries to contact Fiona online, but his wife is suspicious ...

Exercise 2

Write up the following scene, making sure you convey the characters' feelings, particularly in the way they handle the necessary physical contact between them, and in their dialogue:

A woman goes into a beauty parlour to get her nails done by the arrogant manicurist. The two women take an instant dislike to each other.

(27)
ADDING BACKGROUND

How much background do you need to your storyline? By 'background' I don't mean description and scenery, but actual details and extras – the things that add colour and flavour to your story. The answer has to be only what is strictly necessary or you'll hold up the action.

Character background

If, as is recommended repeatedly in this book, you get to know your main character really well before you begin the story, you will be aware of a lot of personal things about him. Things such as how he looks, when and where he was born, how he was brought up, what type of person he is, what job he does, etc. You won't, of course, use it all in the story, but knowing about it will be a great help when filling in his background. Because, even in a really short story, you do need to reveal a certain amount about him or the reader will have trouble empathising with him. And, however exciting the plot, if the reader doesn't care about the main character he will lose interest in the entire story.

Look at the motives of your protagonist. Ask yourself whether you have included enough information about his past life, plus his hopes and dreams, to make his actions credible. Have you given him enough background and, if you are satisfied that you have, are you certain that his experience of life covers it? For instance, if you make him a vet, is he old enough to have completed the training?

The difficulty is in knowing just how much character background you need. Suppose, for instance, you are writing about a son from an immigrant family and his parents are opposed to him marrying out of his religion. It might be tempting to go into how his parents came to be in the country, their difficulties with the culture, etc., especially if you have knowledge of that situation. But, for such a storyline, we would not need too much background – what is important is what is happening *now*. Just a 'slice' of flashback to help us to understand would be sufficient. Beware of trying to inform the reader of everything that happened BEFORE the start of the story. Often it is not relevant to the storyline. Readers are not that interested in the past – the passive part of the story. Give them just enough of it – the vital background – then get back to the present and what is happening now.

Example:

'There's no way I'm going to uni, Dad. I'm getting a job!'

Gary stared at his son. How did you convince such a clever lad that he was chucking opportunity away? Especially when he, himself, had left school at sixteen. 'You'll regret it, Jack—'

'Well, you've done all right!'

Gary shrugged. Carpentry was OK – it made him a living, but photography was his passion. He sometimes wished he'd done a bit more studying. 'You've a lazy streak, Gary,' his wife was forever saying. And she was right.

The amount of background you need depends on the plot, of course. If it is vital for the reader to know that the character cannot run very fast due to an injury, the author has to find a way of getting that fact over early in the story or novel. Such background can be brought in through dialogue or action, or even in thoughts. And try not to add it all in one great chunk – it's better to thread it through the story. But do check that it is crucial.

Plot background

You, the author, will know the plot 'inside out', as it were. It is as clear to you as things going on in your own life. But is it clear to the reader? Are you sure you've covered everything? When the story is finished, go back and make certain the detail is clear. Is the outcome credible? For example, in one of my own stories I had a father telling a stranger all about a family tragedy within minutes of them meeting. Unrealistic, to say the least! It needed more background, more conversation, to put the father at ease before he would have mentioned such a tragedy. The editor picked up the error and asked me to add 200 words. Those 200 words made the plot much more credible.

Even if you have a word limit and are fighting to keep to it, essential plot background must go in. If you are already up to the word count (for a competition, for instance) you will have to lose those 200 words elsewhere. Not easy, but possible.

MASTERCLASS EXAMPLE

He fumbled for her name but she supplied it.

'Katherine Hodge. I was your secretary when I worked here three years ago.'

Pat knew she had once worked with him, but for the moment could not remember whether there had been a deeper relation. It did not seem to him that it had been love – but looking at her now, that appeared rather too bad.

'Sit down,' said Pat. 'You assigned to Wilcox?'

(from 'Teamed With Genius', a short story by F. Scott Fitzgerald)

TOP TIP

Beware of repetition. Check that you haven't made that point about the character's background elsewhere in the story. Is it already obvious, perhaps through his dialogue, thoughts or actions?

ADDING BACKGROUND – THE MAIN POINTS

- Relevant background helps the reader to identify with the main character
- Check that you've enough, yet not overmuch
- All background information must be crucial to the story

Exercise 1

You are about to write a short story about two sisters. The following plot points are central to the story and need to be in at the start. Write the first page, bringing in Sally's background. Use dialogue, thoughts and action where necessary.

Sally is sixtyish, has never married and is mean with money. She has to go to visit her older sister, who is ill. The sisters fell out years ago and Sally resents having to go …

Exercise 2

A name will often conjure up a certain type of character in your mind. Pick a name from the following list. Give that person a problem and write a paragraph about them, bringing in vital background information as economically as possible.

- *Geoffrey*
- *Tara*
- *Lucy*
- *Peregrine*

(28)
CREATING EMOTIONAL REACTION

Experienced authors, using their own unique style of writing, often turn most of the general advice on its head. But in this section we come up against the one absolute rule that is rarely broken: *your story must transfer an emotional experience to the reader.* That is the whole point of fiction writing. Readers often read fiction because they are missing certain emotions in their everyday lives and turn to the writer to fill that need. They want to feel something at the end of your story: anger, love, pity, or perhaps a whole range of emotions.

Readers must also experience the characters' emotions; how they feel towards each other. They don't, of course, analyse why they are reading. Yet often it is not just for entertainment but to be moved emotionally.

What type of emotion?
Before writing any fiction, authors should decide clearly which dominant emotion they want the reader to feel towards the characters – particularly the main characters – by the end. It is easy to be vague and think, 'I want the reader to feel sorry for Alec and be happy for Fay.' That is not enough. You, the author, need to be passionate about getting emotion across, or you will not convey it to the reader.

What are some of the major emotions?

Love	Grief
Hate	Happiness
Fear	Pity
Anger	Hope

There are also the so-called secondary ones, which can be exaggerated and used as themes. Emotions such as:

Jealousy	Despair
Loneliness	Boredom
Greed	Guilt
Courage	Amusement

There are, of course, many more. And remember that whichever emotion you aim for, there is another 'must' for the reader – satisfaction. Even if the story ends tragically you want your reader to think: 'How sad! Yet it could not have ended any other way.' If an ending suits the story, the reader is satisfied.

Before you begin to write, give some thought to emotions:

• Those you wish to create in your characters towards each other

• Those you wish your reader to feel towards each of the characters

• Those you wish your reader to feel himself at the end

What are the most effective ways of showing emotion? As an example, let's take a situation. Liza's husband has just left her. We could write this in several ways.

Telling the reader
When Max left her, Liza felt she just wanted to die.

This method, just coldly stated, is not to be recommended. How can readers feel anything at all, either within themselves or for Liza when they are told in that detached way? There is no emotional impact there; the author is just stating facts.

In Anne Tyler's novel *The Beginner's Goodbye*, Aaron's wife, Dorothy, has died. The story is told in the first person from the widower's point of view and this is Tyler's way of getting emotion across: *And then the laundry, exactly twice a week – once for whites and once for colors. The first white load made me feel sort of lonely. It included two of Dorothy's shirts and her sensible cotton underpants …* That piece makes the reader feel deeply for Aaron.

There are instances when you have to just 'tell' about the emotion. Perhaps you need to get unimportant information over and move on. But it is far better to open up the scene and show it if you can.

Showing the reader through thoughts and feelings

The door slammed and Liza sat rigid, unable to move. Then the truth dawned. Max had gone. What now? Angrily, she brushed away large, salty tears. How dare the man do this to her?

Here we see and feel for Liza – we are in her viewpoint. The scene is brought to life through her thoughts and, importantly, through her feelings.

Showing the reader through dialogue

'Max walked out on me,' Liza said, her voice breaking.

'Never!' Beth gulped over her coffee. 'I don't believe it!'

'What can I do, Beth?' Liza sobbed. 'How do I go on?'

That passage shows how both Liza and Beth feel – by the words they say and how they say them. Of course, you are only able to get emotion over through speech if you have other people present. But what people say can add so much to their character.

Showing the reader through action

The door slammed. Liza sat in silence for ages, unable to move. Eventually, the pungent smell of overcooked meat forced her to get up. In the kitchen, she began to laugh hysterically. A whole chicken … what would she do with it? Picking up Max's redundant knife and fork from the carefully laid table, she hurled them at the wall.

This way the author invites the reader into the situation and allows him to draw his own conclusions. It can be a really effective way of showing emotion because readers have to work out things for themselves. Clarity is paramount.

Whichever way you choose, you are more likely to involve the reader emotionally if you write from inside the viewpoint of the character concerned. (See (10) 'Understanding Viewpoint'.)

Using the senses

Sensory appeal such as *tingling fingers*, *the tensing of calf muscles*, *dry mouth*, *trembling in fear* and *tears of joy* help to bring out emotion in character and reader alike, but most of these are clichéd expressions. Try to be more original.

Emotions to curb

Excessive suffering. If you need this in your novel, keep it as brief as you can. Whatever you want readers to feel – pity, or glee that 'a baddie' has got their come-uppance – they will be reluctant to suffer in detail along with that character, good or bad. The same goes for excessive cruelty to animals. Primarily, people read a book for entertainment.

Self-pity. If you want your reader to sympathise and admire your character, never allow that person to be self-pitying. The minute your characters feel sorry for themselves, any sympathy your reader was beginning to feel for them will vanish. Just as it does in real life.

MASTERCLASS EXAMPLE

She walks into the bathroom and turns the hot tap on full... . As the room fills with steam, she stands in front of the mirror.

You'll never see him again, she tells herself. The places where he touched her – her neck, her lips and her arm – seem raw, almost painful. She looks herself right in the eye, daring herself to cry. Then she presses her hand against her shirt, over her heart, and says, in what she thinks is a strong yet offhand voice, 'I never want to see you again.' She can detect only the slightest quickening in her heart's beat, only the faintest tightening of her throat. She'll have it perfect by tomorrow.

(from *After You'd Gone* by Maggie O'Farrell)

TOP TIP

After you have written a sad scene or story, reread it and analyse your own feelings. How moved are you? You should, at the very least, be on the verge of tears. If you, the author, are not involved, how can you expect your reader to be?

CREATING EMOTIONAL REACTION – THE MAIN POINTS

- What emotion do you expect your reader to feel by the end?
- Show the emotional reaction, rather than tell about it
- Don't forget to use the senses

Exercise 1

Select one or more of the following phrases, which 'tell' of an emotional state, and rewrite them in a few sentences or a paragraph. Dramatise them by 'showing' the emotion. Use action, dialogue or thoughts – or a combination.

- She felt exhausted
- He really hated his boss
- Granddad came home drunk
- She had fallen in love with the man next door

Exercise 2

1. Write a paragraph characterising a likeable person by showing his or her emotions. Use action, dialogue, thoughts – or a combination of whatever is necessary
2. Now characterise a real villain in the same way

(29)
APPLYING HUMOUR

The usual plea, from editors and publishers alike, is: 'We don't get nearly enough humour! Plenty of gloom and doom, but not much funny stuff!' So, why is that? Authors will say that being funny is notoriously difficult. Yet we all have a sense of humour. But people laugh at different things. A joke or comical story that one person thinks is hilarious can leave another stony-faced. So, if we don't all laugh at the same things, how can we write a humorous story that will have everyone in fits of laughter? The answer is that we can't. We have to accept that humour has many parts and, like happiness, it is impossible to define.

How do we attempt to write a funny story or novel? It goes without saying that you are more likely to succeed if you are a natural comic and always see the funny side of life. The humour of a situation is going to come more naturally to you and so, of course, will the words you need to make it comical. But let's suppose that – though you have a brilliant idea for a humorous piece of fiction – you are not a laugh-a-minute type of person. Will it be too difficult to tackle? No! Just accept that, while yours may not be a laugh-out-loud, hilarious book or story, it will be the uplifting 'quiet smile' or 'chuckle to yourself' type. And that type of fiction can be just as funny and satisfying – or even more so.

Don't force it
Forced humour that does not come naturally is rarely that funny. Putting in specific jokes or going over the top with some situation just to get a laugh might work, depending on the idea and the writing, but not often. It is better to let any humour develop as a result of the storyline.

If you set out to write a humorous novel or short story, it doesn't have to be one continuous laugh. Indeed, it cannot be. The reader needs to come up against some serious moments amid the comical stuff. P.G. Wodehouse is an example here – even in the hilarious chapters there are anxious moments. And alongside the funny antics of Charlie Chaplin, there is real pathos. It is worth remembering the fine line between comedy and tragedy – the people in the funniest situations are often really vulnerable. Del Boy and Rodney, in TV's *Only Fools and Horses*, are two such characters.

At the other end of the scale, if you set out to write a heavy, serious novel, you will need to lighten it now and again.

Characters

If your main characters are basically funny or eccentric people you might feel you are halfway there in the humour stakes. But not necessarily. The temptation will be to go over the top as regards action, dialogue, etc. And always remember that even funny or eccentric people have still got to be credible. OK, this is fiction, so perhaps you can allow them to be a bit larger than life, but they must be *believably* funny. Otherwise your reader will shrug, label the person 'silly' and lose interest.

One way to make your characters funny is to make them different. Try giving them an obsession or trait. A horror of cats, a passion for old radios or a love of baked beans – anything really extreme will suffice. Odd traits give rise to possible humorous situations. Another thing that works well is this: if you have made your main character really colourful and 'wacky', try putting him with some seriously dull people. The eccentric person will stand out. Contrast, in comedy, is important.

Setting

You might think a joke shop, a firework factory or a space ship would provide funny backgrounds. But, often, putting characters in a setting that people know well – so that they can imagine themselves in the situation – works best. If you have created really funny characters, try putting them against a straightforward, ordinary setting, say a supermarket, an office, or whatever. And vice versa: surround serious characters with a more bizarre background.

Dialogue

If you have created humorous characters, you can have fun with their dialogue.

Here, Aunt Patty, living in a Residential Home, has a visitor:

Patty frowned at the girl; it was 'Goose', her niece. Patty called her that because there was no way the little mouse would ever say 'boo' to one.

'So, Aunt, what did we have for lunch today?' Goose ventured timidly.

'Stew! Overcooked and over-rated!' Patty shouted, pulling at her bright pink cardigan and thumping her chest. 'Terrible indigestion – I intend to sue!'

Contrast of characters here helps to exaggerate Patty's eccentricity.

First person humour

If your storyline demands a light, humorous tone, you may find that using the first person viewpoint (*'I laughed'*) will work better than using the third. You, the author, can get right under the 'I' person's skin and emphasise his character. It will help to give the story a lively, immediate feel and the reader, too, will find it easier to identify with 'I'. This can only add to the humour.

Example in the third person:

He pranced on to the stage, feeling really embarrassed in the long dress. Any minute he'd fall flat on his face. Panto Dame, indeed! He felt more like a prize idiot.

First person:

I pranced on to the stage in the stupid long dress. Talk about embarrassed – any minute and I'd fall flat on my face. Some Panto Dame! Prize idiot, more like …

When you use first person you can take more liberties with the text than in the third, because you are right into the person's thoughts. You can cut sentences, rearrange them, make them funnier: *Prize idiot, more like* is more amusing than *He felt more like a prize idiot.*

First person, present tense, can work even better, making the scene really vivid and sharp:

I prance on to the stage. Wow, how embarrassed can you get! And I am about to fall flat on my face. Some Panto Dame! Prize idiot, more like …

Short sentences and lively dialogue add a light touch, as does alliteration – using the same initial letter for subsequent words. Titles can be especially amusing in this form. A title such as 'The Motivation of Maisie Miller' might work on two counts. One, it succeeds in indicating that the ensuing story is likely to be humorous – and two, it sets the tone of what is to come.

A word about punctuation. Writing humorous material does not give you licence to 'pepper' the page with exclamation marks. It has been said that over-use of these can give the impression that the author is laughing at his or her own jokes. Food for thought …
Anyway, it is a fact that a sentence usually comes over funnier with a mere full stop at the end, leaving any humour to the reader's intelligence and not emphasising it by !

MASTERCLASS EXAMPLE

Eva delayed marrying Brian for the three years of their interminable courtship because she kept hoping that he would light her sexual spark and make her desire him, but the kindling was damp and the matches spent. And, anyway, she couldn't face abandoning her maiden name, Eva Brown-Bird, for Eva Beaver. She had admired him and enjoyed the status afforded to her at university functions, but the moment she saw him standing at the altar, with his hair shorn and his beard gone, he was a stranger to her.

As she reached his side, somebody – a female voice – said in a loud whisper, 'She'll not be an eager beaver tonight.'

(from *The Woman Who Went to Bed for a Year* by Sue Townsend)

TOP TIP

Using dialect in dialogue will often make that person's speech funnier. But add it sparingly – too much will irritate readers not familiar with the idiom from that part of the country.

APPLYING HUMOUR – THE MAIN POINTS

- Never force it – producing a quiet smile, rather than a loud 'Ha! Ha!' will often suffice
- Contrast of character, situation, background, etc., will help enormously
- First person viewpoint works well

Exercise 1

Eccentric, 70-year-old Bill has an obsession with one of the following:

- *Songs of the Sixties*
- *He takes in stray dogs and his house is full of them*
- *His immaculate lawn*
- *A horror of motorways*

Pick one of the above and work out a humorous plot involving Bill and his obsession. Then write some hilarious dialogue between him and another character.

Exercise 2

Using first person present tense, write a humorous paragraph on one of the following situations:

- *A belly-dancing class*
- *A customer in a butcher's shop. She is besotted with one of the assistants*
- *A single lady of 80 is left to care for her neighbour's two-year-old son in an emergency*

(30)
ESTABLISHING SETTING AND ATMOSPHERE

Setting – where the story takes place – will probably change as the plot progresses. As well as giving the reader background, it creates atmosphere and mood. Thomas Hardy's novel *The Return of the Native* opens with the whole of the first chapter describing the landscape of Egdon Heath. That setting evokes a wonderful atmosphere and the description is superb, but would it work in contemporary fiction? Today's readers are usually impatient to get on with the main story.

Yet, though lengthy descriptions can be tedious, stories can also fail through the *lack* of setting. In the short story, with its restricted word limit, this is understandable. Understandable, but unwise. Readers need a sense of where the main action is taking place, along with some vital atmosphere to draw them in, or they will get confused or bored. Sometimes just a couple of lines are all that is needed. Setting is part of the story. It also helps to mould character and create emotion. Think of it as a necessary part of the plot, giving important background to the action.

In F. Scott Fitzgerald's novel *The Great Gatsby*, Jay Gatsby stands out as a character mainly because of his integration with the book's setting: the Jazz Age. The whole novel is steeped in the atmosphere of the Jazz Age. Indeed, most of the classic works of fiction succeed principally because of where they are set. Charles Dickens' wonderful characters come to life in nineteenth-century England. In *Wuthering Heights*, Emily Brontë used the windswept Yorkshire moors. In most successful stories or novels you cannot imagine the characters in a different setting.

Yet the story must always come first. Never allow your setting to dominate your story but don't forget it, either. Whilst you are showing all that exciting action, remember that the reader might need a reminder now and again of where this is all taking place. Setting gives stability to the action.

Real or fictional settings

Should we always write about only what we know? New writers tend to worry whether or not they should write about an actual building, town, street or landscape. A lot depends on the story. You might be really keen to write a novel set in America, though you have never been there. Is that wise? However much research you do, might you not get something wrong? What about the smell and feel of the place? You can't get that from books or the Internet.

Or maybe you can. I once complimented a successful writer on the authenticity of her novels, set in the United States. She replied that she had never been to America. It was all done through studying books, films and television. (No Internet, back then.)

Another way to use a setting you are not familiar with is just to suggest it. In other words, don't delve too far into that part of your character's life. Supposing he works in a factory, an abattoir or a bakery and you haven't a clue what goes on in those places. You could just use one or two key facts and leave it at that. But, of course, you can only 'cheat' in that way if the job is not that important to the plot.

You might decide to use a setting you once knew well. If you were born in that town and are really steeped in its history, you think you are familiar with the feel, smell and atmosphere of the place. But things are changing all the time. Get one little detail wrong and someone will be on to you and your publisher immediately. Go back to your home town and check the facts before you send the manuscript out. Remember the old adage: there is always someone who knows more than you. The route the majority of authors take is to perhaps use and name an actual area, say Dorset or Cornwall, London or Dundee. They then go on to make the important aspect in the plot – the town, street, church, library – fictitious. It is safer.

Setting and character

Setting can help enormously with characterisation. The house, flat, caravan or boat that people live in, along with their possessions, can reveal such a lot about them.

Example of an opening lacking setting:

Jean sighed contentedly; it was so beautiful here. Then she frowned, the peace suddenly shattered by a crowd of young teenagers messing about at the water's edge. She should leave; the noise and the heat was getting to her. She wished now that she had joined Gaynor on that trip. So good of her daughter to bring her on this holiday …

We really could do with a setting there. Jean is on holiday. Where? On a beach in Italy, by a hotel pool in Wales? If we are to get involved with her story we want to be able to visualise her somewhere.

Ullswater … Jean sighed contentedly; it was all so beautiful. Sitting here on the shore you could easily imagine Wordsworth striding through the trees dreaming about his daffodils. Then she frowned, the peace suddenly shattered by a crowd of teenagers messing about at the edge of the lake. She should leave – their shrieking, plus the searing heat, was getting to her. She wished now that she had joined Gaynor on that Windermere boat trip; so much cooler on the water. Good of her daughter to bring her to the Lakes …

As well as putting Jean in an actual place, we also learn a bit about her character as she thinks about Wordsworth, etc. Also the senses are used and they can play a big part in evoking atmosphere. Here we 'see' the beauty of the place, along with the imagined daffodils; we also get the sound of the shrieking contrasting with the peaceful place and feel the 'searing heat'.

Some landscapes, like this one, can be uplifting, others depressing. Depending on the mood you wish to evoke in your story, you can use setting to add to the atmosphere. It can also, of course, be used to contrast mood.

Don't neglect to mention the weather which can be really significant alongside your setting. For instance, if someone was really down because of a break-up in a relationship, they might see the pouring rain as dreary or the windswept moors as overwhelmingly bleak. But suppose they had just fallen in love? They are then likely to have a different take on the rain and maybe dance in the puddles. Lovers might view the windswept moors as romantic in a Brontë-like way.

MASTERCLASS EXAMPLE

It was dark in the coach now, for the torch gave forth a sickly yellow glare, and the draught from the crack in the roof sent the flame wandering hither and thither, to the danger of the leather, and Mary thought it best to extinguish it. She sat huddled in her corner, swaying from side to side as the coach was shaken, and it seemed to her that never before had she known there was malevolence in solitude. The very coach, which all day had rocked her like a cradle, now held a note of menace in its creaks and groans.

(from *Jamaica Inn* by Daphne du Maurier)

TOP TIP

Don't be tempted to go into terrific detail when you describe your setting. Through watching television and films, modern readers are familiar with such places as courtrooms, prison cells or the canals of Venice. They need the *atmosphere* of the place, rather than a geography lesson.

ESTABLISHING SETTING AND ATMOSPHERE – THE MAIN POINTS

- Place your characters in a setting as soon as possible in the story
- If you use a real place, check and recheck your setting
- Amid all the action, the reader might need a reminder of the setting

Exercise 1

In around 500 words, write the beginning of a story about a man or woman on their first day in a new job. You choose the job. The setting will be the premises – shop, office, factory, hospital, or wherever. Concentrate on the environment, remembering to use the senses. Show the person's reaction to their surroundings.

Exercise 2

In no more than fifty words, describe one or more of the following settings. Don't forget the senses.

- A vet's waiting room
- A doctor's surgery
- A shoe repair shop
- A museum
- A hairdresser's
- An actor's dressing room

(31)
PROVIDING ESSENTIAL DESCRIPTION

No human being ever spoke of scenery for above two minutes at a time, which makes me suspect that we hear too much of it in literature.

(Robert Louis Stevenson)

The word 'essential' is crucial here. Suppose you have spent some time writing a longish piece describing the landscape; the fields, the river and the mountains in the distance. Poetical, you might call it, having taken great care over the words. But is it all really necessary? You might need a little to create atmosphere and background, but too much 'fine' writing can distract the reader from the story.

Every time you describe something in detail – the view, a piece of furniture or perhaps a character – you don't just slow the pace, you actually *stop* the story. Fiction is action – description is static. Some, as we have said, is essential, in order to paint a picture for the reader – where is the story taking place, where does the hero live, what does he look like? But description works so much better if it is threaded in with the action and dialogue throughout the story, rather than plonked in all in one go. So keep it brief and never describe something that does not need describing.

Character description

A brief description of the person is usually necessary, if only to help with characterisation. It is very easy for authors, who have probably 'lived' with their character for ages, to overlook the fact that they have not described him to the reader. Something about his appearance and character deserves a mention. But, rather than tell us *Janine was aggressive,* let's see her being aggressive, perhaps through dialogue:

'Janine, don't talk to your mother like that—'

'I'll say exactly what I like!' Janine declared. 'She's not bossing me about – no way!'

(See (33) 'Making Appearance Count')

Description of place

Readers today will not stand for long paragraphs of description. It is better in small doses, threaded through the narrative. Brevity and selectivity are important. Try adding it to the action or reveal it in someone's thoughts. Or show it in dialogue: *'Wow, look at that gorgeous view! Fields stretching for miles …* ' or *'I'd love to be able to sketch that church. See the intricate architecture over the door?'*

You cannot always do it like that and you may find you have to describe a scene in a straightforward, omniscient way. If you do, watch out for overuse of adjectives and adverbs. (See (37) 'Using Adjectives and Adverbs'.)

The senses

Description usually involves at least one of the five senses: sight, sound, touch, taste and smell. Show them from a character's viewpoint and you will arouse an emotional response in the reader. Let the character feel the wind stab at her face or the oppressive dampness of the caves. Or, in this instance, taste the food:

Harry gasped as the hot spices exploded in his mouth. Eyes watering, he swallowed the curry. Wow! His tongue seemed to be on fire.

Compare that with:

Harry took a mouthful of curry. The food was much too hot and spicy.

MASTERCLASS EXAMPLE
The beginning was simple to mark. We were in sunlight under a turkey oak, partly protected from a strong, gusty wind. I was kneeling on the grass with a corkscrew in my hand, and Clarissa was passing me the bottle – a 1987 Daumas Gassac. This was the moment, this was the pinprick on the time map: I was stretching out my hand, and as the cool neck and the black foil touched my palm, we heard a man's shout. We turned to look across the field and saw the danger. Next thing, I was running towards it.

(the beginning of *Enduring Love* by Ian McEwan)

TOP TIP

A brief mention of the person's clothes can help a lot when it comes to description: *Peggy glanced down at her black skirt and sensible shoes. She would surely shine, unlike the other overdressed applicants.*

PROVIDING ESSENTIAL DESCRIPTION – THE MAIN POINTS
- Description is static. When you use it you are stopping the story. Keep it brief.
- Try to thread essential description in throughout the story, rather than in large chunks
- Cut excessive adjectives and adverbs

Exercise 1

Write the opening of a short story. Two friends are sitting on a bench overlooking a beautiful view. The husband or wife of one of them has just died and that person is being comforted by the other. Reveal their conversation whilst also threading in, either through thoughts or dialogue, comments about the scenery. Remember that the view must take a 'back seat' to the main story of the bereavement.

Exercise 2

Using around 250 words, describe one or more of the following actions. Restrict adjectives and adverbs, but make what could be a boring scene as vivid as possible.

- *Making a cup of tea or coffee*
- *Buying potatoes*
- *Watering the garden*
- *Cleaning the kitchen floor*
- *Brushing your teeth*
- *Making the bed*
- *Feeding the cat*
- *Having a shower or bath*

(32)
MAKING YOUR CHARACTERS REACT

Character reaction is showing how your character feels about something that has happened in your story, or revealing their response to what another character said or did. Reactions are the lifeblood of your fiction. If you don't show enough of your character's feelings and responses your story will fail. That sounds a bit dramatic, but it is true. Be aware, though, that you can show too much reaction, or the wrong kind.

Reaction to events or dialogue is vital because it is the way we build emotion, both in our characters and our readers. Readers want to know how the person at the hub of the story feels at any given time. It is so easy for authors, who are really close to the character themselves, to omit reaction altogether or to skip over it. They forget that their readers have not been 'living' with those people in the intense way that they have. So they might just allow the character a sad sigh or an exclamation and then move blithely on with the story. But the reader must be able to pick up on the person's feelings in order to empathise with him. So, is a sigh enough reaction?

How much reaction?

Unfortunately, it is too easy to overwrite this type of emotion so that it comes across as a bit melodramatic. There are lots of clichéd ways of expressing reaction:

Her legs felt like jelly
He shook his head fiercely
Her heart thumped loudly
He laughed mirthlessly

He clenched his fists
She slammed the book shut
His shoulders slumped
Her lips curled

Try to avoid hackneyed expressions such as these and find another way of showing your character's feelings. Don't be satisfied with the first tired cliché that comes into your head. Spend a little more time on it and you will produce writing of a higher quality.

Sometimes it is better to underwrite. Silence, or very little reaction, can express a great deal of emotion.

Example:

'We've booked for all of us to go to Italy in August,' Dad declared. 'Won't that be great?'

'Super!' Janette cried. 'Can't wait!'

Guy said nothing.

'Guy? What d'you say?'

Guy shrugged. No way was he going to Italy on some family spree.

'Well?' His father was getting impatient now.

Guy cleared his throat and tried looking defiant. It didn't work …

Physical reaction

What are people's main reactions when they are faced with physical conflict? Fight or flight, you might say. Because actual fighting involves some physical act such as a gunfight, fistfight, brawl or a duel, the usual reaction is to hit back, to retaliate. But people also run away from the fight, or hide. Also, if characters are frustrated or despairing, they can react in all sorts of physical ways – by leaving home, ending a relationship, changing their job.

But reactions will not always amount to major physical action. There are lots of smaller, significant ways of expressing emotion. If you want to convey irritation, for instance, your goal must be to make the reader feel as annoyed as the character feels: *Joan scraped back her chair. Dave's fingers, drumming away on the table: dum de dum, dum de dum, was driving her mad. 'I'll wash up,' she declared, and left the room.*

Your story could be about a weak person who is too timid to change their mundane way of life and is stuck in a rut. By the end, something happens to alter their attitude.

Reaction through thoughts

This is when you get right into the mind of the character, showing his reaction to what someone has said or done. We learn of his frustration, shock or whatever, how he feels and what, if anything, he might do about it.

Example:

The lounge was a tip – ransacked. For a minute she just stood there, numb. Chairs overturned, settee slashed, carpet littered with God knows what – all her ornaments and bits and pieces smashed. Unbelievable … why would someone do this? Her legs suddenly weak, she sank to the floor.

Reaction through dialogue

This is possibly the most dramatic, entertaining way of showing reaction – whilst also moving the story on.

Example:

Helen faced a furious Anne.

'Your Katie is dangerous!' yelled Anne.

'Really?' Helen retorted. 'And what of your little darling?'

She glared at Anne. Deep breaths, Helen, she told herself. Don't get too worked up.

'My Molly wouldn't dream of hitting anyone. She's just not like that!'

'Right!' Helen was seething. 'How d'you account for these bruises?'

Grasping Katie's arm, she pulled the child towards Anne. 'See?'

Anne stared. Then she burst out laughing. And all Helen's vows of keeping calm vanished.

'You cow!' she yelled. Making a grab for Anne's hair, she missed and toppled forward.

That dialogue, whilst showing Helen's reaction, also incorporates thoughts and physical action. Sometimes you can thread reaction into an active scene. It can serve as a diversion or a lull amid the action.

Example:

Dazed and shocked, Sharon lay on the floor where Keith had left her. Minutes later, she tried to move, but her arm was killing her. The police

... she should phone. She began to crawl across the room. The photo of Rob, in its smashed frame, stared up at her. Rob – if only she had never met the man. Painfully, she edged to the door.

Sometimes you need to get across the fact that, though the character appears to be showing one particular reaction, in his mind there is a completely different type of emotion going on.

Example:

As usual, he found himself laughing at his wife's silly jokes. Ruffling her hair, he inwardly congratulated himself on his casual manner.

'And how was your day?' he smiled.

'OK,' she answered. 'And yours?'

'The same,' he said. But suddenly all he could see was Clare's sensuous face this afternoon. He looked away, just in case something in his own expression revealed a bit too much.

MASTERCLASS EXAMPLE

... I could not say why I had laid out the vegetables as I did. I simply set them out as I felt they should be, but I was too frightened to say so to a gentleman.

'I see you have separated the whites,' he said, indicating the turnips and onions. 'And then the orange and the purple, they do not sit together. Why is that?' He picked up a shred of cabbage and a piece of carrot and shook them like dice in his hand.

I looked at my mother, who nodded slightly.

'The colours fight when they are side by side, sir.'

(from *Girl with a Pearl Earring* by Tracy Chevalier, set in 1664)

TOP TIP

Write some notes about your main character before you start the story. (See (14) 'Getting to Know Your Characters'.) Knowing him well will ensure that any reaction you give him later will suit his personality.

MAKING YOUR CHARACTERS REACT – THE MAIN POINTS

- Reaction is the way we build emotion, both in our characters and our readers
- You know your character well. But have you put in enough of his reactions to bring him alive for your reader?
- Often the most revealing reactions are those that are under-written

Exercise 1

The following are all over-used, clichéd reactions. Substitute your own original phrase.

- *She gave him the cold shoulder*
- *A teardrop squeezed from her eye*
- *He lowered his gaze*
- *She went as red as a beetroot*
- *She felt tired out*
- *He went berserk*

Exercise 2

In a paragraph, write a reaction – in dialogue, action, thoughts or a mix of the three – to one or more of the following situations. Use your own words, rather than clichéd expressions.

- *A party intruder ... from the host's viewpoint*
- *An aggressive patient ... from a nurse's viewpoint*
- *A stroppy teenager ... from the mother's viewpoint*

(33)
MAKING APPEARANCE COUNT

Getting across your main character's outer appearance is important. 'But,' you say, 'my story is only 1,000 words – there's no space to go on about how she looks!' True – there has to be real economy of words if you are writing the 'short, short' story. Only the really essential words will do. Yet it is imperative that you find room for at least one aspect of the main character's appearance. In women's magazines – the main market for short stories these days – readers like to 'see' their characters to be able to identify with them and become really involved. And they can only visualise them if the author gets across how they look, how they walk, how they are.

Describing characters

Straightforward description, especially at the beginning of a short story: *He was tall and thin with grey eyes and a pompous manner,* rarely works. You want your reader to have an idea what he looks like, yes, but concentrate on the characteristics that are relevant to the story. Maybe his sight is impaired and that plays an important part in the plot, so try to show it early on.

Suppose the whole point of your story rides on the fact that your main character, a young lad, has red hair and is being bullied at school because of it. The red hair needs to come in early in the story. You could bring it in like this: *Ethan ate his porridge quickly, avoiding looking at the photo of himself on the sideboard. All grins and red curls – ugh! One day he'd smash it.*

If you are writing in the first person and need to get the heroine's appearance over, how do you do it when she is alone in the room? Often, authors have her stare in the mirror, then think or say something like this: '*My hair is too long. And going blonde doesn't suit me.*' Though that works, the method has become very clichéd. Try to get her appearance across in another way, perhaps through someone's dialogue later in the story: '*Why don't you change back to brunette, Alice? It suits you better than blonde.*'

In a novel you have more time and space. The way characters look can emerge more gradually. Don't leave it too late in the story, though – we've all read books where we imagine the hero to be dark-haired and slim, only to discover on page 90 that he is fair and stocky!

Show, rather than tell

'Telling' is stating someone's appearance in a straightforward way:

Tara was attractive with long blonde hair and blue eyes. She was also overweight, with no interest in fashion.

If possible, it is better to 'show' how Tara looked. The four main ways you can 'show' are through:

- Dialogue
- Thoughts
- Emotional reaction
- Action

Put Tara in a situation, show how she looks using any – or all – of the above ways.

Example:

'*Tara, where did you get that awful top? It's much too tight – makes you look really fat!*'

Tara glared at her mother and shrugged. She knew she was overweight, but she didn't really care, not now Ian had left her. Tossing back her blonde hair she slouched off.

That paragraph SHOWS how Tara looks and also how she feels. It is more interesting that way and doesn't hold up the storyline with a straightforward description. (See (19) 'Showing Instead of Telling')

> **MASTERCLASS EXAMPLE**
>
> 'He's nice,' Julia said, 'he has curly black hair.'
>
> Aunt Maureen and Julia's mother stared at her, their expressions similar, a mixture of barely suppressed curiosity, and distaste.
>
> 'Curly black hair?' Aunt Maureen queried, as though curls in themselves were deeply suspect in a man.
>
> Julia nodded. 'Sometimes,' she said, 'he ties it back in a ponytail.'
>
> Stunned silence.
>
> 'Not with a ribbon,' Julia added hastily, 'just with an elastic band, I think. Iris likes it tied back.'
>
> (from *The Unknown Bridesmaid* by Margaret Forster)

TOP TIP

Having created the character, you, the author, are naturally familiar with his appearance. But the reader is not. Check that you've added enough about his looks and personality to make him come alive for the reader.

MAKING APPEARANCE COUNT – THE MAIN POINTS

- Appearance aids identification
- If possible, show rather than tell
- If word-restricted, select one striking aspect that sums up the character

Exercise 1

Bring the following character to life in a paragraph. Show her appearance by creating a situation. Use dialogue, thoughts, emotional reaction or action – or perhaps a combination of all four aspects.

Penny was attractive, in a lethargic, dreamy way. Tall and thin, she tended to be quite clumsy. She never hurried and took ages to do anything.

Exercise 2

Becky needs to describe John, her new boyfriend, to her pal, Pam. From the following description, show how Becky gets John's character across to Pam, all in direct dialogue.

John is dark-haired, has no self-esteem and is average-looking. He tends to lark about and tell old jokes to overcome nerves, but people see through him.

(34)
MAKING SMOOTH TRANSITIONS

A transition denotes a change of scene or a lapse of time in your story. In a novel it can also herald a change of viewpoint. It is the link between scenes – when you need to get your character from A to B quickly. Think of it as a hinged door through which the story moves forward to get into another room. The transition – the door – is not important to the story but the reader needs to know it is there.

Transitions are necessary because a writer cannot, alas, just tell his story from beginning to end in a chronological sequence. He has to move it from one place to another to show what is happening now and he also needs to use flashback in order to reveal what happened before. Then there are the dull but essential parts of the story, such as the character's routine and the passing of time. Transitions of time, place and, often, viewpoint all have to be included. The author has to decide how these are to be done – whether they need a lot of space or just a line, and to answer that you have to decide how important to the story they are. Also, whichever transitions are made, they must be executed well or the reader is in danger of being jerked out of the emotional suspense of the story.

Road signs

You need to put in a 'road sign', keeping the reader aware of the passage of time. Often, it can be simply done, like this: *Two hours later …* or *The next day they met again …* or *Meanwhile, on the other side of town …* There is nothing wrong with that method of moving your story on. Those phrases serve as a bridge and denote clearly that you are now about to move on in time. But, should you need to deal with the character's feelings or have a lot of changes of scene or time lapses, you might need to find a smoother way of doing it.

Also, using too many expressions such as *The next day ...* or *Later, they ...* can read like sloppy writing. Should you be about to tackle a completely different storyline – a new viewpoint and a change of setting and content – then start a new chapter.

'Between the lines' transitions

Often a transition can be done with just a 'white space'. This is when, about to change scenes, the author leaves a space between sections, indicating that the story has skipped a stretch of time. You may not even need a gap, especially if just a short period of time has passed, so long as it is clear to the reader. And often it is good to leave things to the reader's imagination and intelligence – he or she can conjure up for themselves what happened in between.

Sex scenes are an example. The genre or market that the short story is aimed at is important here; usually too much detail is not welcomed by editors of women's magazines, for instance. Also, if the characters have been skilfully and sympathetically drawn, readers will fill in the gaps themselves.

Unobtrusive transitions

Fiction must seem to be continuous action and, though the actual 'door' may not constitute vital action in the novel, the way you deal with it is paramount. Poorly done transitions can confuse the reader. One effective method is to throw in clues. Mention something in one paragraph and then follow it up after the time gap.

Example:

She asked him to pick up the wine from Tesco's on the way home. A useless request – he never remembered such things.

But, surprise, surprise; at six thirty he walked in and plonked a bottle on the table.

If you do it that way, you have moved the story on – jumping the hours which are not important to the story – and the main plot continues, uninterrupted by time.

Another method of galloping through time, if you want to move the story on really quickly, is like this:

The first day Don left, Jill felt terrible, really devastated. A couple of days later, anger had taken over and by the end of the week she was actually enjoying her freedom.

That way the time lapse is almost unobserved – skipped over, because the author wants Jill, with her range of emotions, to recover swiftly.

Emotional transitions

If your character has changed emotionally during a transition, you might need to enlarge upon the 'why' and 'how' later in the story. Take the situation with Jill, in the above example. Her reactions were quickly dealt with over the period of a week. But if, after the transition, a little explanation was needed to make the transformed Jill credible, it could be done in flashback:

Thinking back to that awful first week, Jill realised that Gyp, her Jack Russell, had played a big part in her coming to terms with things. Don had always ignored him – and did she really want to live with someone who didn't like animals?

Flashback is a good solution there, showing how Gyp helped with Jill's recovery.

MASTERCLASS EXAMPLE

It was three days later when Eva saw the car for the second time, a moss-green '38 Ford parked outside the Pepperdines' house. Before that it had been outside Miss Knox's and Eva knew the car belonged to neither Miss Knox (an elderly spinster with three terriers) nor the Pepperdines. She walked quickly past it, glancing inside. There was a newspaper and a map on the passenger seat and what looked like a Thermos flask in the door pocket on the driver's side. A Thermos flask, she thought: someone spends a lot of time in that car.

Two hours later she went out 'for a stroll' and it was gone.

She thought long and hard that night, telling herself initially that if she saw the car a third time she would move out.

(from *Restless* by William Boyd)

TOP TIP

Rather than writing *Several days later ..., After some weeks ..., A few years before ...,* the use of actual times can be far more effective: *On Tuesday at seven o'clock ..., Three weeks later ..., Two years earlier ...* You might need to plot more accurately, but being precise instead of vague will score dividends.

MAKING SMOOTH TRANSITIONS – THE MAIN POINTS
- Think of them as doors: you have to get to the next room (scene)
- Keep transitions smooth and, above all, clear
- Put in a clue before the transition and pick up on it afterwards

Exercise 1

A father is working away. His wife phones to ask him to bring home a birthday present for their young son. He forgets to do so. There is a row and the father storms out of the house. He comes back later with the gift. The house is empty. There is a note from the wife, who has left with the son.

At which of these points would you use a quick transition:
- *The wife phoning*
- *The row*
- *His trail around the shops to buy the present*
- *His reaction when he comes home from the shops*

Exercise 2

Improve on these transition phrases:
- *After a few days ...*
- *Later, when they met ...*
- *Soon afterwards, she felt better ...*

(35)
MOTIVATING YOUR CHARACTERS

What motivates your characters? What makes them act and react in the way they do? In other words, what makes them tick? Perhaps the most important thing to consider, before you answer those questions, is what type of people they are. You, the author, have created and developed them as the story progressed. So when they face a dilemma, a decision or even an emotional reaction, you should know them well enough to get it right. For instance, supposing you make your character impatient and aggressive at the beginning of your novel, building him up into a real bully in the middle. The reader, expecting an explosion of some sort around him – a murder or, at least, a fight – will feel cheated if he mellows and the excitement fizzles out. Unless, of course, you give a good reason for the change.

Suppose your main character – let's call him Roger – is a timid, rather weak man who likes a quiet life. If Roger walks into his local shop to find the owner on the floor and someone robbing the till, he is likely to turn tail and run, rather than confront the robber. When you show your character as a particular type of person his motivations must match his personality. Now, it might suit your story for Roger to suddenly become brave and bash the robber over the head, making it more dramatic and exciting – but it would not be credible, any more than it would be if you had created Roger as a dare-devil hero yet, faced with the same situation, he turned and ran away.

What you have to remember is that you are addressing all types of readers. Some of them are innocent people who will always believe almost anything they are told. Others will take an awful lot of convincing in order to believe anything at all! So, to cater for everyone, it is better to give your characters adequate and believable motivation. Ask yourself, what is the most typical and logical thing that type of person would do in these circumstances? Then you will be believed and readers will go along with your story.

Believable motivation

Now, surprising things do happen in real life – we have all done at least one crazy thing in our time. And writers will quote these extraordinary happenings, insisting that it is entirely possible that a person in a story could suddenly act completely out of character. 'But it actually happened like that in real life!' they cry. And, yes, you might read in the papers that a lovable, gentle soul has murdered his wife because she was too besotted with her pet dog. Or that a guy, terrified of heights, has scaled a tall building to rescue a child.

If someone in real life does something contradictory, or without motive or reason, we are amazed by it and we might talk about it. But we will not disbelieve it – because we know that it definitely happened. It is true! Fiction is not – if you have your character do something incredible, without motivation, the reader realises that the whole thing is phony and loses interest. He or she cannot suspend disbelief and believe the story any more. So your characters need to be typical, ordinary people who 'flow with the tide'.

The only way you can allow someone to do something completely out of character is if you have prepared the way earlier in the story. Perhaps some experience makes them see things differently and therefore they act eccentrically, but there would have to be a strong, well-motivated reason. It must be logical that they would act in that unusual way. You cannot make your character act illogically or do something without adequate reason just because it suits your story at that point. Readers will not accept such an easy way out.

So your characters must have motivation for pursuing their goals. In most stories the main characters will have worthy motivations for acting as they do. They act out of such motives as:

- Love
- Justice
- Duty
- Dignity

Below are some examples:

Situation	Motivation
A mother resolves to help her son kick his alcohol addiction	Love
A detective is looking for a murderer	Justice
A daughter gives up her career to care for her sick mother	Duty
A pensioner won't accept cash benefits he is entitled to	Dignity

There are, of course, negative motivations:

- Revenge
- Greed
- Hatred
- Lust

Using a negative emotion as an overriding trait in your main character is not likely to work as well as giving him a 'worthy' one. Readers have difficulty in sympathising with a character whose goal is to get even with someone. Such a person might be dubbed an antihero and, as well as being more difficult to create, books and stories with antiheros as protagonists are more difficult to sell. There are, of course, notable exceptions: Zoe Heller's novel *Notes On a Scandal* is one. But Heller was careful to give her 'I' character, Barbara, some good points; loving her cat was one.

You do, of course, need to give all characters negative motivations at times – after all, without such hitches there would be no story! But, often, using a more positive main motivation works better – especially if you are writing for the commercial short story market. Editors prefer uplifting tales that pursue a so-called 'worthy' intention.

MASTERCLASS EXAMPLE

... but when I saw (John) *lift and poise the book and stand in act to hurl it, I instinctively started aside with a cry of alarm: not soon enough, however; the volume was flung, it hit me, and I fell, striking my head against the door and cutting it. The cut bled, the pain was sharp ...*

'Wicked and cruel boy!' I said. 'You are like a murderer – you are like a slave-driver – you are like the Roman emperors!'

'What! What!' he cried. 'Did she say that to me ...'

(from *Jane Eyre* by Chralotte Brontë)

TOP TIP

Ensuring that your characters' motivations are credible does not mean that the characters themselves have to be stereotyped. Create an unusual protagonist, by all means. Just be sure that you give him logical motivation.

MOTIVATING YOUR CHARACTERS – THE MAIN POINTS
• Ask yourself – would he or she really do that?
• The motivation must be logical
• A 'worthy' motivation is more saleable

Exercise 1

Select one activity or pastime you did yesterday. What was your motivation for doing it? Write 200 words on the purpose behind it and what motivated you. If you merely watched TV or cooked a meal you can still do this exercise. Why did you choose that programme ... or that particular meal?

Exercise 2

Pick one of the following situations. Write a paragraph showing the motivation for the person's action. Make it a strong, logical motivation – one which could be the basis for a short story.

1. *A man goes into a pub for a rendezvous with a guy he fell out with years ago*
2. *A girl who has not seen her mother in years decides to get in touch*
3. *A timid child seeks out a teacher she dislikes*

(36)
ENSURING CLARITY

In fiction, clarity is everything; writing is all about communication. Beautiful prose, an amazing plot, natural dialogue and perfect structure are all pointless if the reader is confused. And sometimes we, as authors, do not realise when we are not being clear. One of the main reasons is that we are too close to the material ourselves. To us, it is perfectly obvious what we are trying to say or do in our story or novel because we have spent hours living with it. It is our 'baby', so to speak. We can easily overlook the fact that we've not spelled out something vital. You might say, 'Ah, but I don't want to patronise readers – some things need to be left to their intelligence.' True, but not at the expense of confusing them. It is far better to err on the side of saying too much than trying to be so subtle that you muddle people.

If – after you have revised your story – you are still doubtful about clarity, get someone else to read your manuscript. This is where a Writers' Circle or group can be invaluable. And it doesn't have to be a writer who looks over it for you – any keen reader will soon point out something that is not clear.

So, what are the main aspects we should be checking?
• Sentence construction and choice of words
• Time and transition
• Dialogue
• Plot sequence
• Characters and viewpoint

Sentence construction and choice of words
We are all familiar with the phrase 'never use a long word where a short one will do', but it is worth repeating here. Short, simple

words aid clarity. Long obscure ones, put in for effect to make the author sound clever, will not work. Contemporary fiction needs to be readable and entertaining, whatever the subject. For instance, if you are writing a historical novel you will have to adjust prose and dialogue accordingly, but you must still keep your readers in mind. Will they understand the jargon?

Check your sentences. Are they too convoluted or muddled?

Example:

Jenny went into the kitchen to attend to the stew which was simmering on the stove, hoping that Tracy would come round to her way of thinking and that maybe her gran would talk some sense into her, but there was not much hope of that because she was in a foul mood and Tracy never took notice of anything anyone said.

That sentence is confusing and would benefit a) from cutting, b) from breaking up into shorter sentences and c) from playing up the important points. Do we really need all that about the stew? Who is in the foul mood, Gran or Tracy? Is the point of the piece given the emphasis it deserves? Better like this:

Jenny went to check on the dinner. Was it too much to hope that Tracy would come round to her way of thinking? Maybe Gran could talk some sense into her. Not much hope when Tracy was in such a foul mood. Anyway, since when had the girl ever taken any advice from anyone?

Time and transition

Is it clear when and where your story is taking place? Make sure you transfer readers smoothly from scene to scene. If you use a flashback, make sure that it is clear you have now gone back in time.

In a short story, try to devise a plot that takes place over as brief a time span as possible. A brief time span works better with the restricted length. It reads more smoothly and is less confusing and jerky. Expecting readers to jump weeks or – worse – years, can jar in such a short piece.

Dialogue

Any confusion with dialogue is usually because the author has not made it clear who is speaking.

Example: (Three men: Bob, Alan and Bill are talking together)

'How's your wife?' asked Bob.

'Fine, gone to her mother's.'

'You're lucky! Mine wants me to take her shopping.'

'You poor devil. Thank God I'm single,' said Alan.

'My wife's gone to a party. I'm not invited.'

'Tough!'

We can identify Alan, but who said the 'shopping' line? Each person's speech should come over individually. (See (15) 'Making Good Use of Dialogue')

Plot sequence

Are your characters' goals clear and does the plot move forward in a logical way? A straight chronological structure is easiest to follow – and easier to write. Readers are unlikely to get confused because they are taken along a straight road without too much deviation. Keep flashbacks brief; they must not distract from the main story, and if you have a sub-plot in your novel make sure it stays that way and does not override the principal one.

If you have any doubt at all about the reader understanding something that you have allowed a character to do or say, you must find a way of explaining it. If you are doubtful about overdoing explanation, one way around it is to go ahead and put in everything you think you need to make the plot clear in the first draft. Afterwards, when you revise and are more familiar with the story, you will see exactly what needs to be cut.

Characters and viewpoint

The short story works better with one main protagonist and perhaps just two or three more characters – fewer, if possible. The main viewpoint character needs to be established immediately, so that the reader can begin to identify with him or her. As stated in (5) 'Choosing your Characters' Names', never use names that sound alike (there are enough to choose from without picking Sharon and Sheila, for instance). Vary your characters in appearance, speech and actions as much as possible, so they stand out clearly as individuals.

Jumping about in viewpoint will also confuse and irritate – better to stick to the one angle in a short story. A novel is different; you often need to change viewpoint and the book can be all the better for it. If you are worried about clarity, why not use the same order each time, so that the reader gets familiar with the changes? For example, you could have three chapters from Adam's angle, then three from Karen's, and so on, keeping to the same pattern throughout.

MASTERCLASS EXAMPLE

I came forward to the head of the stairs and stood there, smiling, my hat in my hand, like the girl in the picture. I waited for the clapping and the laughter that would follow as I walked slowly down the stairs. Nobody clapped. Nobody moved.

They all stared at me like dumb things. Beatrice uttered a little cry and put her hand to her mouth. I went on smiling, I put one hand on the banister.

'How do you do, Mr de Winter,' I said.

Maxim had not moved. He stared up at me, his glass in his hand. There was no colour in his face ...

(from *Rebecca* by Daphne du Maurier)

TOP TIP

If you give a sentence too many focuses it makes it confusing. Think of each sentence as having just the one purpose. Your writing will be sharper and clearer.

ENSURING CLARITY – THE MAIN POINTS
- Keep words and sentences simple
- Keep flashback brief and time sequences clear
- Unless the story calls for it, do not try to be too subtle. Clarity is everything

Exercise 1

Rewrite the following piece. Cut the long sentences and make it clear who is saying what by using direct dialogue. Cut what is unnecessary and emphasise the important aspects.

Dan told his grandson to go out with his friends because he was playing his rock music too loud and he was fed up with it but Kyle ignored him. He went to the kitchen and broke a few eggs in a pan because he was hungry and got out a plate and knife and fork. Kyle stood there staring at him and he thought he should ring his daughter and tell her that he'd decided to go and live with his son in New Zealand because he couldn't stand it here any more, what with the weather and Kyle and also the blessed dog which yapped all the time.

Exercise 2

Rewrite the following dialogue giving each speaker an individual style (mild, aggressive?) so that it is clear who is speaking without adding 'he said' or 'she said'. Make the piece come to life! Decide on their characters, relationship and ages before you begin.

'I'm going out.'
'I don't think so.'
'Well, I am.'
'There is housework to do—'
'I'm not doing it.'
'You are.'

SECTION FOUR:
ADDING
EXTRA SPARK

(37)
USING ADJECTIVES AND ADVERBS

Adjectives

Pepper the sentence with too many adjectives (the describing words) and you'll weaken it. The reader will just skip over the adjectives to get to the noun, and all those descriptive words will end up being superfluous. One is usually enough. Better still, cut them all and use one good verb.

Example, using two adjectives:

She looked up at the huge, majestic mountain.

Example, using one effective verb:

The mountain towered above her.

In that second example, a powerful verb – 'towered' – is used to good effect. You don't need adjectives like 'huge' and 'majestic' – the verb 'towered' gives a stronger feeling of the mountain 'looking down on her'.

Cut unnecessary adjectives:

An **acute** crisis	**Undue** hardship
A **terrible** disaster	A **serious** danger

Are any of the above adjectives (in bold) necessary? For instance, a disaster is surely just that – a disaster. We know it is terrible.

An example of using too many adjectives:

Entering the tiny terraced house, Cheryl peered at the scruffy, peeling wallpaper in the gloomy hallway. Already she felt depressed and claustrophobic in the small, box-like hall, which smelled musty, damp and unwelcoming.

First of all, do we need 'tiny'? It is a terraced house, after all. And 'scruffy'? If the wallpaper is peeling we don't need to be told it looks scruffy. The adjective 'gloomy' is fine – the reader is now picturing the hallway through Cheryl's eyes. We are told that she feels claustrophobic, so do we need 'small' as well as 'box-like' to describe the hall? The words 'musty, damp and unwelcoming' together are clichéd.

The piece is better like this:

Entering the terraced house, Cheryl peered at the peeling wallpaper in the gloomy hallway. Already she felt depressed and claustrophobic in the box-like hall. There was an odd smell like old mushrooms – a damp smell, which made her shiver.

When you revise your writing, watch for all unnecessary adjectives and cut them. Try to find a more interesting way of describing something. Sometimes it can be done through dialogue or action or, as in Cheryl's case, in her thoughts. The verb is the important word – always use a good verb in preference to too many adjectives.

Adverbs

In the same way, beware of using unnecessary adverbs – those little creatures that usually end in 'ly'. The most unnecessary use is in qualifying dialogue – adding a word to 'he said' when you've already shown how he or she feels by their speech.

Example:

'I didn't mean to hurt you,' she said apologetically.

Or

'That'll show you!' she said gleefully.

Look again at those two sentences. In both cases we know how she feels – it's all there in the words she says. So we do not need the two adverbs 'apologetically' and 'gleefully'.

This also applies to action scenes. Are the adverbs necessary in the following phrases?

*She sobbed **loudly***

*She panicked and ran **desperately** from the room*

*She tried to give the baby a bottle, but he still screamed **incessantly***

Whenever you use an adverb, check that you've not already indicated that 'ly' word elsewhere. If the writing is clear and visual, you should not need it.

MASTERCLASS EXAMPLE
Between seven and eight in the morning and between two and three in the afternoon, the German planes punctually come to drop bombs. They fall just about everywhere, without causing much damage or casualties. But the bombing and the response of our fighter planes and anti-aircraft guns, my, what a din it makes!

(from *Earthly Paradise* by Colette)

TOP TIP
Don't feel you can never use adjectives and adverbs. Your story may need some; just use them sparingly.

USING ADJECTIVES AND ADVERBS – THE MAIN POINTS
• Use a good verb and dispense with adjectives where possible
• You should not need that adverb to qualify the dialogue. The dialogue itself is paramount.
• The use of too many adjectives and adverbs becomes ineffective. Readers fail even to notice them.

Exercise 1
Rewrite the following passage, cutting any unnecessary adjectives or adverbs. Try to find good, relevant verbs to put in their place.

Dave peered critically at himself in the large, imposing mirror on the wall. After coming through all that heavy, teeming rain his dark, wavy hair was lying flat against his head. He groaned loudly at his reflection and turned away quickly. The gorgeous, sophisticated Sally would surely run a mile when she saw him …

Exercise 2
Imagine you are writing a short story and must cut it right down.

There are 46 words in the scene below. Rewrite it in 23 – using half the words – or less. Cut all unnecessary adjectives and adverbs whilst still keeping the visual effects.

The wide green fields stretched as far as the eye could see and Jane spotted a high church steeple in the far distance. A lovely scenic view, but the menacing black clouds above spoiled the beautiful summer scene. Jane began trudging reluctantly down the winding lane.

(38)
JAZZING UP THE WRITING!

This is an exercise to do right at the last minute, after you have completed your revision. Go over the manuscript just once more. This time you are aiming to add a little extra – a spark, that touch of magic that will make your work stand out from the rest. First, if it is a short story, print it out. Having it in your hands to read gives you a different impression. Working on the computer screen, where you can so easily change things, can sometimes make you a bit careless. In print, words hit you with more force than they do on the screen.

If it is a novel, print out the excerpt that you felt doubtful about when you did the read-through. Maybe, though you've polished it over and over, you thought things went a bit flat at that point? Print out anything you feel could be livened up or improved at all, whether it is a full chapter or just a scene.

Now read the piece through. Could you – even at this late stage – find ways of improving it? Could you do something to make the manuscript stand out from the rest? OK, we all say we could go on for ever revising and we have to draw the line somewhere. But just check the following aspects before you submit the manuscript.

Cut the clichés

Clichés do nothing for your writing style except make it look tired. Phrases such as: 'at the end of the day', 'when it comes to the crunch', 'the mighty oak', are so mundane and boring that they hardly register any more. Finding a new way of describing something can only add life to your writing.

Be positive

Write what was, not what was not! If you have had to use gloomy or depressing material, have you avoided too much negativity? 'The road ahead was black and eerie' is better than 'There were no street lights'. Or 'She was upbeat about the interview', rather than 'She was not worried about the interview'. Anything that helps to lift both the writing and the subject – whatever the content of the story – is good.

The senses

The senses can add so much to the writing – have you remembered to use them? Sight, hearing, touch, smell and taste can do so much to jazz things up. When you are rereading your work ask yourself, did you really *feel* that sweaty hand, *taste* that lemon meringue …

Colour

Have you used colour to good effect? 'He spotted her lime green jacket at the back of the queue,' or 'He spotted her at the back of the queue.' Which sentence gives the best picture? Colour is so often omitted, yet it – literally – brightens any story and brings scenes to life. Supposing you have your character hugging her cat. What colour is the cat? We want to picture her with her pet and some colour brings the scene to life.

Be specific

This follows on from 'colour' in that you will improve your writing no end if you are specific in what you are writing about. The cat, above, for instance: is it long-haired, short-haired, oriental? Even if the animal is not that important to the story, 'her black Persian' sounds more interesting than 'her cat'. In the same way, 'pasta' is better than just 'food', 'oak trees' better than 'trees' and 'poodle' better than 'dog'.

Adding humour

That grim scene that goes on for a while, is there any way you could contrast it? This is easier in a novel, of course, because you have more space. You may be able to lighten it with a sub-plot, if you have one. Or with the characters; people do the scattiest things in the most serious situations, often out of embarrassment or to enable them to cope.

Split over-loaded sentences

Have you tried to get too much information into one sentence? Great long tirades that make you want to gasp for breath in the middle are a real 'turn-off'. They are also more likely to be confusing. Split the sentence into two and your writing will be that much sharper.

Emotion and passion

Do you feel your main character is strong enough to carry the story? If not, are there any touches you can add here and there to make him stand out?

> **MASTERCLASS EXAMPLE**
> At last, liveried in the costume of the age, Reality entered the room in the shape of a servant to tell the Duchess that her carriage was waiting. She wrung her hands in mock despair. 'How annoying!' she cried. 'I must go. I have to call for my husband at the club ... If I am late, he is sure to be furious, and I couldn't have a scene in this bonnet. It is far too fragile. A harsh word would ruin it ...'
>
> (from *The Picture of Dorian Gray* by Oscar Wilde)

TOP TIP

Never add spark to your manuscript at the expense of clarity. If you are in any doubt that 'jazzing up' the writing might confuse the reader, don't do it.

JAZZING UP THE WRITING! – THE MAIN POINTS

- Aim to 'lift' your story above the rest
- Cut or change anything convoluted or boring
- Aim to surprise and stimulate

Exercise 1

Jazz up the following piece. Try shortening sentences, using the senses, adding humour, being specific about food and flowers, changing the names and adding colour. Use direct dialogue to liven it up.

John eventually came in very late in the evening and when she heard the door shut Mary did not move from the settee and instead shouted at him, asking him where he had been and when she saw his new jacket covered in mud she got even angrier. John stood there grinning and swaying about thrusting a bunch of her favourite flowers at her and Mary realised he was drunk so she went to the kitchen raving that she'd made him his favourite meal.

He laughed, saying he couldn't eat a thing so she threw the plate, food and all, at him and it went all over the wall.

Exercise 2

Think of new phrases in place of these clichés:

- *Her eyes shone*
- *In this day and age*
- *At this moment in time*
- *When the chips are down*
- *I shall leave no stone unturned*
- *She was grasping at straws*

(39)
KEEPING UP TO DATE

Is your contemporary story twenty-first century material? Most of us, at one time, have been guilty of dragging an ancient manuscript out of a file. Needing a short story for a competition and in a rush to meet the deadline, we recall that gem we always liked but never sold and just send it off. Of course, we don't win with it. And we don't deserve to.

Old short stories and novels, submitted as they were originally written, belong in the wastepaper basket. At the very least they will need freshening up and, even if the idea is still bang up to date, there is bound to be something that needs altering. The way people act, react and speak, for instance, is changing all the time. Editors or judges will quickly spot an old manuscript; an editor once told me that she could smell the dust! If it is a historical story you still need to check that the style and language will suit today's readers.

So, how do we make sure our work is fresh and up to date? With a short story, you might think that because the magazine you are aiming at tends to be a bit old-fashioned, anything cosy will do. It will not. Done-to-death subjects are taboo with every potential market today. Even if the magazine tends to print homely stories about nice people, the successful ones will be slick, modern and well written. The editor's priority is *original,* professional stories, written with her regular readers in mind. Study the latest copy and note how the author has used modern technology, brand names, etc. Contemporary novels, too, need a fresh angle with bang up-to-date research and a twenty-first century feel.

What to avoid

- *Soppy heroines.* Strong, feisty main characters work better, both in the short story and the novel.
- *Old-hat short story plots.* Boy meets girl, they overcome a slight problem and all ends happily. *Or:* Heroine inherits cottage from aunt and eventually pairs up with the handsome guy next door, who is still conveniently single (and not gay). You need much more originality today.
- *Coincidences*, in any fiction. They seem a lazy way out of a situation.

Staying in touch

Be aware that your so-called modern idea might be out of date by the time your work is published, especially if it involves technology. Devices such as mobile phones can be an asset for writers but they can also be a menace. Once, we could put people in panic situations with no means of communicating but now, of course, they would have mobile phones. Unless there is no signal …

Mentioning brand names like Tesco or Gap will help to give your work an up-to-date feel, so long as you don't write anything contrary about them. It pays to research the latest fashions and Christian names. (See (5) 'Choosing Your Characters' Names') Make your heroine an engineer, a scientist or a bus driver today. Modern stories are not all happy-ever-after tales but it is still advisable to leave the reader with a note of hope. Keep words, sentences and paragraphs short. Dialogue must be bang up to date, but take care that the slang or whatever won't be dated by the time you are in print.

Young people's dialogue is an example. You can probably let your teen character repeat words such as 'like', because that trend has been around for ages and seems to have stuck: '*I really wanted to go and see Mike but I was, like, too scared to go.*' Trying to be too up to date, though, is not wise because what young people say and how they say it changes so much. Also, your teenager might not be that trendy. Often it is better to show the rhythm of speech, making it sound young and ensuring that it contrasts with the way older characters speak.

Modern fiction needs, above all, to be sharp. Browse libraries and bookshops and read contemporary books in your genre to see what publishers are looking for. Some authors, when writing, prefer to stay away from others' work, but it is important to get a feel for what is up to date in your particular field.

MASTERCLASS EXAMPLE

The aeroplane wheels touched the runway, jerking me awake.

'I envy you, that's a gift.'

The blonde woman in the next seat smiled. I wiped a hand over my face.

'Sorry?'

'You slept like the dead all the way from Tegel. You're lucky, I don't sleep like that in my own bed.'

Some other time I might have asked how she slept in strangers' beds, but I kept my smart mouth shut and waited while the pilot bumped us into a smooth landing, just another flight. The seatbelt lights turned off and the business types got to their feet ...

(the beginning of *The Bullet Trick* by Louise Welsh)

TOP TIP

Eavesdrop on people's conversations and take notes, especially from teenagers' and children's speech. Twist boring mobile phone chats – ask yourself 'What if ... '

KEEPING UP TO DATE – THE MAIN POINTS
- Read good, contemporary authors
- Use modern names, jobs, technology, etc., to bring your story bang up to date
- Never use a clichéd plot

Exercise 1

Root out a favourite unsold short story from way back and *completely* rewrite it, bringing it up to date. The names, language and setting will probably all need changing. Maybe you could rewrite it and send it away?

Exercise 2

Novel plot: *A middle-aged man's wife has died. Ten years ago, he and his wife had a massive row with their teenage daughter – she left home and has not been in touch since. His wife had always refused to try to find her. He has no other family, so now decides to look for the daughter.*

Write the first couple of pages of the novel, concentrating on a contemporary setting, up-to-date language and technology. Give the story a really modern feel.

(40)
CONSIDERING STYLE

The dictionary defines style as a 'manner of writing or speaking'. Writers tend to worry about it and they really do not need to. 'How do I develop one?' they ask. The answer is that your style is you and, to a certain extent, is already there. It is individual to you and your personality, and the more you write the more it will grow, shaping itself as you work. Everything about you defines your style; your childhood, adult influences, your friends and jobs. Indeed, the way you live your life. So, there is no need to worry about developing your basic writing style. But you will, of course, have weaknesses within it – we all have – and, once you are aware of them, it is possible to correct your faults and strengthen the good points.

Help to shape your style by reading the best authors – particularly those who produce the type of story or novel that you want to write. And practise, practise, practise, in order to improve your sentence construction, use of words and, indeed, everything else about your writing.

Belonging to a serious writing group and having your work read out anonymously is a really good way to learn about style and improve it. If you have been attending for some time, your individual style will have emerged and, even if you are asked to write something quite alien – a crime story when you usually write romance – your style will often still be recognised.

Polishing your style
Style is not something extra that you add to your story. It is something that is already there but it can often be heightened at the revision stage, usually by cutting, rather than adding.

Can you change your style? Basically, perhaps not, but you can certainly bend it a little, if you need to. For instance, if you want to write commercially and your style tends to lean towards being a bit heavy with a slow-moving plot, you are probably going to have to lighten it to suit your market. That is quite possible. You simply dress up or dress down the story, accordingly. Let's look at that literally. You are invited to a formal party, but normally wear casual stuff and are not keen to dress up. But, if you really want to go, you will compromise. It's the same with writing – if you want to sell, you will write to suit that market.

Voice

Style and 'voice' are often intertwined, but there is a difference. Your style is what brings about your voice. Think of style as your basic character and your voice as the way you use words, dialogue, sentences, etc. Authors such as Hemingway and Chekhov had their own distinctive voice, as do contemporary authors such as Sue Townsend and Salman Rushdie.

The more writing you do, the quicker your own individual voice will develop. In the meantime, concentrate on making your writing as entertaining as possible, style-wise. Avoid monotony and give your story or novel lots of variety. You can do this in small ways – using direct dialogue or varying sentence and paragraph length are examples.

Sentences

Example 1:

Kerry was aware that she looked a right mess as she dragged herself from the water.

Revised:

As she dragged herself from the water, Kerry was aware that she looked a right mess.

What is the most important part of that sentence? Is it that Kerry thinks she looks a right mess? If so, as the end of the sentence tends to make more impression on the reader, it is more effective if changed around.

Example 2:

Stuart grinned into the faces of his audience and hurried from the stage.

Revised:

Grinning into the faces of his audience, Stuart hurried from the stage.

Opening with 'Grinning' (the present participle), works better, making the action seem more intimate.

Think about your sentences, the words you have used, the dialogue, the reactions of your characters, the way you have dealt with description. They seem small things but if you improve them you will enhance your style no end. If it suits the story, getting right into your character's viewpoint so that the reader can identify emotionally with him or her will also help. As will using the senses, qualifying vague words ('apple trees', instead of just 'trees'), adding colour and cutting anything unnecessary. It will make all the difference to the finished story or novel. (See also (38) 'Jazzing Up the Writing!')

MASTERCLASS EXAMPLE

Cornelius tears off a piece of bread and dips it into his soup. He chews for a moment. 'My dear, I have something to discuss.' He wipes his lips with his napkin. 'In this transitory life do we not all crave immortality?'

I freeze, knowing what is coming. I gaze at my roll, lying on the tablecloth. It has split, during baking, and parted like lips. For three years we have been married and I have not produced a child. This is not through lack of trying. My husband is still a vigorous man in this respect. At night he mounts me; he spreads my legs and I lie there like an upturned beetle pressed down by a shoe. With all his heart he longs for a son ...

(from *Tulip Fever* by Deborah Moggach, set in seventeenth-century Amsterdam)

TOP TIP

If you are just starting to write fiction, it is probably better not to try to do complex, experimental or so-called 'literary' stories until you have developed your own style. You will find it easier to write in the usual straightforward way, with the protagonist wanting something and getting it – or perhaps not – by the end.

CONSIDERING STYLE – THE MAIN POINTS
• Your style is individual to you
• Add touches to enhance it at the revision stage
• Read the best authors and practise, practise, practise

Exercise 1

Take your favourite book, classic or contemporary, preferably one written in the style you would like to develop yourself. Copy out (preferably by hand) a page of what you consider to be excellent writing. Afterwards, you will see far more quality in that passage.

Exercise 2

Make the following sentences more interesting:
• *Mesmerised, she stared at him as she walked towards him*
• *The chair was knocked to the floor with a thud*
• *Bill was sure that he could win the game and tried once more*

(41)
MAINTAINING TENSION AND PACE

Tension is what keeps us reading. If there is no tension, with one trauma adding to another, we won't really care what happens at the end. So why read on? **Pace** is the rate at which the story moves along and covers time, action and movement. Both of these aspects are important – tension and pace are the glue that holds the story or novel together. And if that glue is not strong enough then the plot will fail.

Tension

The best way to create tension in a story or novel is, to use a cliché, to raise the stakes. Your main character has a problem and is striving to overcome it. How do you keep the tension going? Certainly not by providing a ready answer there and then. Do that and the story is over. No, you need to put an obstacle in the way of solving the first problem so that things get worse, then something else happens to get in the way of him solving it, and so on, depending on the length of the story. You have to keep your readers biting their nails, worrying about the poor character and wondering how he will ever get over his psychological trauma or break away from the gang, or whatever. (See (3) 'Developing A Plot')

When you plot, try to ensure that each approaching 'obstacle' will be larger than the one before. If you don't, the landscape will level out, as it were, and the reader – hoping for more excitement, not less – will be disappointed. The story needs to build up and up. Think of Alfred Hitchcock's film *Psycho*. The tension in that was unbearable – and not just in the shower scene. Hitchcock, dubbed 'the master of suspense', managed to stretch the tension almost unendurably throughout the film. He never let up and the film was a lesson in how to get the most out of tense situations. If we can do that in our writing we will certainly keep our readers biting their nails … and buying our books.

Of course, you need a really strong, intriguing situation or setting to put your characters into, then you can begin to wring what you can out of it. One way of stretching the material is to set the scene then slow it right down, perhaps with dialogue, thoughts or description. Terse sentences will add to the tension.

Example:

Her heart thumping, Susan took a step back.

'Don't worry, sweetheart,' the man said.

Susan could hardly breathe. How had he got in? She had locked the doors. He smelled foul as he lurched towards her.

'Pretty little thing,' he smirked, stretching out a large, rough hand.

'Get out!' she yelled.

You could make that even longer if necessary, building more suspense. Even if someone is alone you can prolong the 'agony'.

Example:

Hours later, left alone lying on the damp, dirty floor, Mia tried to stay calm. The gag around her mouth was stopping her breathing and the ropes cut into her wrists. Why had Bruce done this to her? Where was she? The wall opposite was covered in graffiti – an old warehouse?

She must go along with whatever he wanted when he came back … or she might not get out alive.

You have to decide how long that scene can go on. How much can the reader take? It depends what led up to it. Maybe, if it is a novel, you can now go into Bruce's viewpoint, leaving the reader in suspense as to Mia's fate. Then return to her angle later. It would add to the tension.

Pace

Pace can mean a lot of things in fiction writing. First, the time aspect. You, the author, control the way time passes for the characters. It must be done smoothly and fit in with the pace and tone of the novel or story. You have to decide which scene needs skipping through quickly and which one needs to be expanded. The story usually signals how to do this: 'She got straight on the bus and was at Dan's in no time,' will suffice if the journey itself is irrelevant. But if you move too quickly through a more important scene the reader will feel frustrated or, worse, confused. Also, if you trundle too slowly through an episode you can bore the reader, who is then likely to skip on to a more exciting chapter.

The material of the book or story should determine the pace. Genres such as adventure, humour or thriller, usually demand a swifter pace, whilst relationship, romance or psychological stories need a smoother, more reflective approach. Think of each scene as though it were a dramatic episode in a play. And remember, as mentioned in the 'tension' section, you want each episode to appear more dramatic than the one before. In a novel, the finale of each scene is a kind of curtain drop, so at the start of the next scene the reader will be expecting time to have passed, and also that there may be a change of background.

Action stories need short scenes which help to quicken the pace. Short paragraphs will also work well, as will sharp dialogue. Too much description, too many flashback scenes and long gaps in time will all hinder the pace. A romance or a psychological or character-based story can be more leisurely, with longer scenes.

Tension and pace are rarely the main issues we consider before tackling a story. But it is essential to get them right.

> **MASTERCLASS EXAMPLE**
>
> … We found him at last on the edge of a shell hole.
>
> 'Ah,' grunted the Major suddenly. He went down on his knees. I crouched beside him, still staring at the back of his jacket.
>
> 'Torch. Hold it right down close to the ground. Here, get round to the other side. Mind the damn hole.'
>
> I felt my way round what was left of the man on the ground. He was quite oblivious to our arrival.
>
> 'Torch. Now, man.'
>
> … the man began to scream again …
>
> 'Run it slowly down his body. I don't think there's much hope … Oh, Jesus Christ.'
>
> (from *How Many Miles to Babylon?* By Jennifer Johnston)

TOP TIP

If you decide to write an 'action' short story, plot it to cover a really short time gap. It will add to the pace.

MAINTAINING TENSION AND PACE – THE MAIN POINTS

- Create more tension by making each problem bigger than the one before
- Suit the pace to the genre
- Keeping to one viewpoint will help to keep the story moving

Exercise 1: Tension

Plot: *A male bus driver with one female passenger drives way off route, right out in remote countryside, and stops the bus.*

Write the dialogue between him and his petrified passenger. Whose viewpoint will you use?

Exercise 2: Pace

Plot: *A policeman chases a thug through the streets and finally catches him. Next morning the thug is interviewed and then released. He has no money so walks five miles home, only to find his mother has been taken to hospital. His sister drives him there and there is a scene by his mother's bedside, where he is upset and guilty.*

How would you pace this plot? Which parts would need to be written at a fast pace and which much slower? And how would you link the scenes?

(42)
CREATING CONTRAST

Contrast is an aspect of writing that we can easily forget. We are usually so obsessed with getting other things right that contrast gets overlooked. By 'contrast' I mean contrasting facts, dialogue, scenery or whatever, wherever you can. Contrasting characters, especially, can produce amazing results – adding sparkle and sharpness to your writing. For instance, if your story is set in an office environment, try adding one eccentric type among all the nine-to-five occupants.

How about giving that elegant shop assistant, working in a posh boutique, a slovenly way of speaking? Or set your grand wedding scene in pouring rain or maybe send your millionaire character to prison. Putting a timid character in a situation foreign to her nature always adds drama to a story. Remember Scarlett O'Hara in *Gone with the Wind*? Author Margaret Mitchell had Scarlett, a pampered Southern Belle, going through experiences completely opposite to her nature, in a war-torn country, at that.

Charles Dickens was brilliant at what you might call 'miniature characterisation', introducing secondary characters and bringing them to life with their contrasting natures. But a word of warning to novelists – don't get too carried away with those weirdly different secondary types. They must not become more important than the main ones. Dwell too long on them and the reader will think: 'The writer is lingering on this odd person, so he must be crucial to the plot.' Only to be disappointed later on, when he realises that that colourful character has disappeared from the story.

The film director Alfred Hitchcock was a master of contrast. He would often stage a gruesome murder in broad daylight – usually in brilliant sunshine – when most of us would have had it happen on a dark, rainy night. Hitchcock's murder scenes seem all the more shocking when contrasted in this way.

Amaze your reader whenever you can – just so long as you don't stretch credibility.

> **MASTERCLASS EXAMPLE**
> ' ... Let me see you play cards with this boy.'
>   'With this boy! Why, he is a common labouring-boy!'
>   I thought I overheard Miss Havisham answer – only it seemed so unlikely – 'Well? You can break his heart.'
>   'What do you play, boy?' asked Estella of myself, with the greatest disdain.
>   'Nothing but beggar my neighbour, Miss.'
>   'Beggar him,' said Miss Havisham to Estella. So we sat down to cards.
>
> (from *Great Expectations* by Charles Dickens)

TOP TIP
Size makes for interesting contrast. If your main character is six foot tall and built like a tank, why not give him a miniature poodle ...

CREATING CONTRAST – THE MAIN POINTS
- Contrast characters, dialogue, weather, scenery, setting ...
- Contrast adds sparkle and surprise to your writing
- Try placing your character somewhere opposite to his normal environment

Exercise 1

Three women and four men are sitting in a doctor's waiting room. From the viewpoint of the receptionist, write a paragraph on each of them. How does she see each individual? Contrast their characters as much as you can.

Exercise 2

Write a paragraph describing how the protagonist in each case copes with a situation they are unused to.

- *A timid person makes herself read a poem at her mother's funeral*
- *An arrogant toff is forced to look after his sister's disabled child*
- *A prim and proper teacher confronts a streetwise thug.*

(43)
SURPRISING THE READER

Surprise is important. Adding or twisting some aspect of your story that makes readers sit up in a 'Wow, I didn't see that coming!' way can only be good. Predictable, but necessary, scenes, dull dialogue, essential but tedious description – it all cries out for that extra something. We all love surprises. Reread those mundane parts of your story – could you bring in an element of the unexpected somewhere? Let someone say something startling or put in another sentence that could raise eyebrows? Small surprises, done sparingly, can add so much. Two short story writers who excelled in surprise endings were O. Henry and Roald Dahl. Dahl's work was used in a TV series: *Tales of the Unexpected*.

Bear in mind that any surprise must be credible. Unless you have shown motivation for him to change, you cannot have your serious character suddenly come out with something completely dotty. Also, your surprise does not have to be a massive happening. A tiny incident, reflection or reaction will lift a story, as will a little unexpected colour. Sometimes just changing a sentence around will do it.

Example:

Viv, sitting in the cinema alone, was shocked to see her ex, Jamie, in the row in front. She tried to concentrate on the film, but it was hopeless.

Better like this:

Viv, sitting in the cinema alone, tried to concentrate on the film, but she was too shocked. The familiar figure in the row in front was none other than her ex, Jamie.

Put that way around, the reader gets more of a sense of surprise. Jamie is the main focus, so he needs to be mentioned right at the end of that sentence for effect.

Endings

Books with unexpected endings often work very well but, because of the length and often complicated content, it can be difficult to hold back the surprise to the end. Such novels need to be carefully plotted and structured before being written, so the format will probably not interest those who never plan. At the end of Daphne du Maurier's *Rebecca*, we are shocked to discover that Maxim hated his first wife, then he confesses to killing her, before it is revealed that Rebecca was dying anyway. There are clues to these twists earlier, but the story is cleverly told from the angle of the timid second wife. Because we are in her viewpoint and she is not the type to work things out, neither do we. Another, more contemporary, example of a surprise ending can be found in Julian Barnes' novel, *The Sense of an Ending*, which won the 2011 Booker prize.

'Red herrings', deliberately misleading clues as used in abundance by Agatha Christie, create a false trail and make the reader suspect the wrong character. But do ration your red herrings – too many can confuse and irritate the reader.

A surprise, of course, can be a negative one. You can have your characters come home after a holiday and find that their house has been burgled. Or a mother gets an email telling her that her daughter has run off with a married man. But any surprise – good or bad, small or large – that makes the reader think 'this is unexpected, what now' has to add to the story. And you, the author, will be respected for putting it in. Surprise your readers and sometimes you may even surprise yourself!

There is a good market for twist-ending short stories, written specifically to surprise the reader. (See (25) 'Creating a Satisfactory Ending')

MASTERCLASS EXAMPLE

'Mr Behrman died of pneumonia today in hospital ... They couldn't imagine where he had been on such a dreadful night. And then they found a lantern, still lighted, and a ladder that had been dragged from its place, and some scattered brushes, and a palette with green and yellow colours mixed on it and – look out the window, dear, at the last ivy leaf on the wall. Didn't you wonder why it never fluttered or moved when the wind blew? Ah, darling, it's Behrman's masterpiece – he painted it there the night that the last leaf fell.'

(from *The Last Leaf*, a short story by O. Henry)

TOP TIP

If you include a completely unexpected happening, such as a fatal road accident, it can sit uncomfortably in the story. Never use it as an easy way out, to conveniently banish a surplus character, for instance.

SURPRISING THE READER – THE MAIN POINTS
• Make sure your surprise is credible
• Use surprise sparingly
• Construct sentences so that the surprise comes at the end

Exercise 1

Finish this passage:

The three people in the railway carriage are nearing the end of their journey. A girl is dozing, her book slipping on her lap, and an elderly gent scans a newspaper. A prim, middle-aged woman stares out of the window and keeps glancing at her watch. Suddenly, a man's voice rings out.

'Don't move!'

A guy, holding a gun and wearing a balaclava, stands at the entrance to the carriage. One passenger yells out in terror, another sits petrified. But the other ...

Which of the characters is the third one? How and why do they react as they do? Surprise the reader!

Exercise 2

Devise a story with a twist-ending, preferably one that – as far as you know – has not been done before. The story is to be 1,000 words or less, so you will not need a complicated plot.

SECTION FIVE:
CONSIDERING VITAL ISSUES

(44)
REVISING YOUR STORY

'Revise? Not me!' some authors say. 'I just write it and leave it!' Others will admit to doing at least seven drafts of a novel, sometimes more. Chances are that both types of writers are successful, so who is to say there is a right and wrong way? The non-revisers will say that their original draft is 'from the heart' and any polishing could deaden the whole manuscript. Yet, often, you find that those people have thought long and hard before they started the story. They will have had a rough idea of where they were going and, if they have the experience and talent, are able to put the words down correctly in the first draft. So it's a different kind of revision.

But, however good a writer you are, there surely must be sentences, paragraphs or parts of the novel or story which need tweaking. Short story writer Raymond Carver claimed to do as many as thirty drafts and never less than ten. We all use different methods. I have a novelist pal who writes one page and polishes it to perfection before moving on. Her gain, of course, is that she avoids lots of revision at the end. This method can only work if you know exactly where you are going and don't change any part of that plan as you write. Alter someone's character even slightly, for instance, and you could be in trouble, unless you jot down notes to remind you to amend things later.

There are the writers who, whether or not the book or story is planned, just 'slap' down the first draft, not stopping until the end. They then spend more time revising than they did actually writing the story! Whilst getting it down, they will not have stopped to worry about anything – sentences, spelling, dialogue, description, etc. For those people that is the worst part over. They feel confident that, though there is a mound of revision ahead, they at least have something to work on.

So we are all different. To help those who do need to revise – the majority of us – the following are some pointers to think about as you reread your story.

Content
What is your story about? Can you sum up the theme in one sentence? The crucial point here is change; what or who has changed by the end? Does the story MOVE? Is there a good balance between action and static scenes? Is the plot credible? Are the time transitions clear and do occasions, such as Christmas, tie in?

The beginning
This can make or break your story. It is the first thing the editor sees. If it is not gripping, has no tension or hint of mystery, will he or she read on? The beginning usually needs a lot of revision to get it right and, because it is so important, I would advise all authors, even those who say they never revise, to recheck theirs.

Whose story?
Is it clear, right from the beginning, whose story it is? Readers like to have a character to sympathise with, so that they can identify with him. If, later, you change viewpoint, is it clear whose story it is now? Have you given the characters motivations for their actions?

Clarity
Difficult, when you are so close to the story, to assess this. A writing group can help so much here. Read aloud any chapters or sections you are doubtful about and they will soon shout if all is not clear. Alternatively, put the story or novel away for a few weeks, then reread it for clarity.

Length

Is the story or novel too long or short to sustain the plot? If it seems drawn out in places it probably needs cutting. Equally, if it appears rushed, the structure is probably not balanced. Market requirements will affect length, of course.

Repetition

Words: Don't strain to find a substitute word for a common one just because you've already used it once. It will show! Yet often you can find a suitable replacement for an uncommon one.

   Content: If you've mentioned it in the narrative, do you really need that character to repeat it in direct dialogue? Cut repetition or you risk boring readers.

Originality

Being original is not easy. But you can check a few things such as stereotyped characters, too many clichés (other than in dialogue), old-hat situations. Find a way round them if you can.

The ending

Is it unexpected, yet believable? Being the last thing people read, it needs to have a powerful impact. A good ending will make the reader go on thinking about the story – its theme, message, etc. And, though it might be sad or leave you wondering, it must never disappoint. A book or story is, after all, meant to entertain.

When to stop revising

This is one of the biggest decisions you will need to make. Sometimes you feel you'll never get it right, but there has to be a stopping point. How much revision is necessary? There is no answer to that. Except that the more writing you do, the sooner you come to realise when you have done enough and you can improve a particular piece no more. Something tells you when to stop. It comes with experience which, I realise, is of no help to beginners. Till you get to that stage, you can always show the manuscript to other writers, who are usually only too glad to help.

Tackling revision

I always do the first and second draft on the computer and then, to revise further, print out the story or novel. Computers might be invaluable for writers, but there is something more natural about checking things on paper. It seems a more intimate and familiar way of working and, after all, this is probably how your work will be read unless, of course, it is on Kindle. Your paper drafts will be a mess because, unlike on the computer, you'll have lots of crossings out and scribble. Old-fashioned and tedious, true; yet more satisfying somehow!

MASTERCLASS EXAMPLE

The first draft – the All-Story Draft – should be written with no help (or interference) from anyone else. There may come a point when you want to show what you're doing to a close friend ... either because you're proud of what you're doing or because you're doubtful about it. My best advice is to resist this impulse. Keep the pressure on; don't lower it by exposing what you've written to the doubt, the praise, or even the well-meaning questions of someone from the Outside World. Let your hope of success (and your fear of failure) carry you on, difficult as that can be.

(from *On Writing* by Stephen King)

TOP TIP

However efficiently you feel you have done your revision, steel yourself to put the manuscript away for at least a few days and forget about it. Then reread it and any errors will jump out at you. Or you could be pleasantly surprised!

REVISING YOUR STORY – THE MAIN POINTS
• Always check and recheck the all-important beginning

- Are the time sequences correct? School holidays, Bank Holidays, etc.?
- Be prepared to cut more than you add

Exercise 1

Revise the following, correcting misuse of capitals, punctuation, etc. For instance, the word 'book' occurs four times and the piece changes from past to present tense.

Jenny wanted to book a trip to london to see the houses Of parliament but her Mother said no, your not going all on your own, dad said your not being fair. She decides to go and books a coach then buys a Guide Book and she read the book before she went.

Exercise 2

Revise this short story beginning, making it more exciting. If you get right into Cassie's viewpoint, showing her terror and making us tremble along with her, the scene will come to life. Let us actually hear those groans!

Cassie did not like sleeping in the creepy house alone. As she went up the creaking stairs she was sure she heard someone groan and knew she would not sleep all night. Then, as she opened the door, she saw a light flash on and off in the dark room, so she went out and shut the door again. She would make a cup of tea and stay up all night.

(45)
DEALING WITH WRITERS' BLOCK

Professional authors will tell you there is no such thing as writers' block. They are trying to make a living from writing, and if they were to wallow in too many so-called 'blocks' their families would suffer. They do have a point – we never hear of accountants' block, bricklayers' block or doctors' block, do we? Novelist Tom Wolfe gives it another name: fear. And maybe that is at the back of it – fear of not being good enough; fear that your next effort will be rubbish. There are two commonly believed myths about creative writing. One is that the muse will suddenly hit you, and the other is that if you wait for inspiration to strike, you will produce a work of genius. Most writers learn about these the hard way. The down-to-earth answer is to apply the seat of your pants to the seat of your chair and write. If only it were so simple …

Why you have writers' block

If you are in the throes of this condition, ask yourself why you feel you can't go on and be honest with the answer. Is it laziness? You thought writing a book would be an easy ride and had no idea of the hard work entailed? If so, just forget about the whole project for a while and do something else. If you really want to write you'll be back later, more prepared for the task ahead.

Maybe something traumatic has happened in your life and you can't concentrate. It will be hard. But, again, think of those professional writers. They cannot allow emotional upset, or whatever, to hold them up. They have to get back to writing, it's their job.

Story content

Apart from psychological reasons or laziness, this is the most likely reason for writers' block. You have no idea how to continue with your story; all imagination and ideas seem to have dried up. This is more likely to happen when writing a novel, because of its length, but the following advice can be applied just as well to short story writers who are stuck. Let's see if we can untangle the cause of why you have become stuck at this particular point and what you can do about it.

Writing block	What to do
You have put your characters in a certain situation that is crucial to the story but can't see a way of getting them out of it. Or you have concentrated so long on this part that you are sick of it – fed up and bored with the whole episode.	*Abandon that scene. Have a go at that other exciting chapter you had planned for later in the book. OK, you prefer to work straight through, but this is an emergency!*
You have run out of steam. Most of the action and conflict you had planned does not seem credible, so you have no idea where to go next with your characters.	*Force yourself to read through the story again. What have you changed to make your original plan unworkable? If you believed in that plan, maybe a rewrite is in order?*
You are bored with the main character and are worried that the reader will feel the same way. You are probably right; if the characters don't come to life the story will not work. So, what is wrong with him? Too stereotyped, too ordinary, too ludicrous, too dull?	*Have you considered changing viewpoint? From third to first, for instance? OK, you will have to do a lot of rewriting, but first person will give a more intimate viewpoint and could really liven up the character.*

Writing block	What to do
The story is coming across far too 'thin', like a sandwich with no meat in the middle. What you thought was a good idea will not sustain 80,000 or so words.	*That original idea needed more plot development before you began. Sounds drastic, but you may have to consider a complete rewrite. Padding out a story is not a good plan. Unlike cutting, it rarely works. Scrap this story and work out a more detailed, 'thicker', plot around the same idea.*

Finding a practical solution
Still blocked?

1. Go and do something physical – gardening, swimming, jogging. Later, look at the story afresh.
2. Give yourself a regular time for writing. After a while, the mind gets attuned to the routine and will 'switch on' at, say, nine every morning.
3. Put the manuscript away (or resist the temptation to bring it up on computer) for at least a week. Then reread it.
4. Study some poetry, listen to music, wander round an art gallery. Then come back to it.
5. Write something completely different, out of your usual sphere.

If you are still in despair, you might try Dorothea Brande's advice. In her book *Becoming a Writer*, she advocates using *the full benefit of the richness of the unconscious*. To do this, she says, *you must learn to write easily and smoothly when the unconscious is in the ascendant.* She advises that you rise earlier than usual and – without talking or doing anything else – begin to write. Write anything that comes into your head, last night's dream, yesterday's events, or whatever. Don't think, just put it down. After a day or two, Dorothea says, you will double your output without trying. The idea is that writing will begin to come naturally to you. And, if Tom Wolfe is right in saying that fear is another word for writers' block, dare I suggest that this simple task might be your answer?

> **MASTERCLASS EXAMPLE**
> You can't wait for inspiration. You have to go after it with a club.
> (Jack London)

TOP TIP

If you don't relish Ms Brande's advice about getting up earlier, try her method anyway, but *anywhere, any time*. Just write – on computer or in a notebook – spontaneously, whatever comes into your head. It could get rid of writers' block!

DEALING WITH WRITERS' BLOCK – THE MAIN POINTS
- Face up to the reason you are in this state
- Do something physical
- Develop a writing routine

Exercise 1

Carry on with the following opening to a story. Try Brande's 'automatic' writing exercise and just write. 'It will be rubbish,' you say. So what – you have written something. Congratulations!

Freya stared at the postmark, not daring to open the envelope …

Exercise 2

Write down why you cannot proceed with your story or novel. Be honest. Would you rather be doing something else, are bored silly with it or has the enthusiasm fizzled out? At least you can now face the reason. Then reread the parts of the story you are quite proud of and do a complete rewrite of the rest.

(46)
LEARNING FROM REJECTION

The first and most difficult thing new writers have to learn is that rejection is quite usual. Being turned down is part of the learning process. Have you ever heard of a successful author who has never had a rejection slip? Most have received enough of the things to be able to paper the walls of their houses (to use an old cliché). One positive side of technology is that if you are rejected by email you can just delete the message, though you do need to keep a record of it. Somehow those 'slips' were more depressing. Also, remember that rejection is not personal. OK, that precious manuscript you have sweated over feels like your baby – 'how dare they turn me down!' – but that editor does not know you. It is just one person's judgment – his or her opinion on that one story or novel.

Editors are only human and personal taste does often come into play, I'm sure. Publisher Michael Legat once remarked that, because he was so fascinated with anything to do with the theatre, he automatically passed any manuscripts with theatrical content to someone else to assess, to allow for bias.

Receiving your first 'thanks, but no thanks' reply is agony. If it is a standard letter or email, with no helpful hints as to why the story was rejected, you think the worst. You must be writing rubbish, what is the point in going on? How come those people at the Writers' Circle said it was good? They've always been so honest; they should have told you to put it in the bin.

Let's deal first with the cold rejection slip that tells us nothing or – perhaps worse – the modern practice of some publications whose policy is: *If there is no response from us after six months you are free to send it elsewhere.*

Part of the learning process

Did you really think you were going to hit the jackpot at the first try? You are learning your trade, after all. Some beginners are under the illusion that, when it comes to writing fiction, there is not a lot to learn. Maybe that is something to do with the fact that most of us have been writing since childhood. By writing, I mean stringing words together competently. Perhaps some would-be authors think that is all there is to it, that we should be able to write well without training, or having to learn any technique. But if you wanted to be an accountant, butcher, or nurse you would hardly be on top of the job without any training, would you? And rejection, in this business, is part of the learning process – honest!

Receiving 'encouraging' rejection slips

A word about standard rejections that come back with added scribbled comments, letters that accompany rejected manuscripts and those encouraging email remarks. Believe me, these are like *gold dust*! Never ignore them. It means that your story was nearly there – someone thought enough of it to put *Good writing, but characters not strong enough* or *Liked this, but not quite the right tone for us.* Editors do not spend time commenting on stuff that is not worth the trouble. Take the remarks *very* seriously. Write another story for that market, but this time act on those comments. Let the editor see how serious you are about writing.

Why was it rejected?

If your manuscript was rejected without any helpful comments you might not have a clue how to improve it if, indeed, it needs improvement. 'It must do – it was rejected,' you say. Ah, but are you aware of the numerous reasons why it could have been rejected (besides the one your pessimistic self has stamped it with – that it is rubbish)? Ponder on this list:

• You hit the wrong market; wrong length, wrong content, etc.

- They have recently accepted a similar story and do not want a replica
- Your English, punctuation and presentation is not up to scratch
- Too convoluted a plot for a 1,000 word story. Or too thin a plot for an 80,000 word novel
- Your over-confident covering letter states that you feel your book is better than some of their published books
- The editor split with her boyfriend last night. Had she read your work two days ago she might have accepted it
- They are snowed under with manuscripts and can accept no more at present

Try again

Unless you had a letter back with your manuscript advising you that there is no hope and suggesting you should take up fishing or embroidery, take heart and try again. One of the best tips I was ever given was, when your short story is rejected, be sure to get it out to another market *that same day.* If it sits around on your desk or on the computer you will just keep seeing 'rejection' all over it. Send it out to another magazine and at least there is hope once more. The snag there, of course, is finding a market to suit.

A few years back there were magazines which took similar stories, lengths, styles, etc., and you did not have to alter a manuscript that much for it to fit in elsewhere. Today there is usually a lot of work to do before you can try another market. Changing a story, to ensure it suits another magazine or online market, is vital. Out of all those reasons for rejection, I have to say that the first one – not right for the market – is probably the biggest cause. (See (48) 'Checking on Market Study'.) So do alter your work and send it out again, or you will never know if that story, which you once really believed in, had potential. With a novel, also, do your research and resubmit it, but only to a publisher or agent interested in that genre.

Par for the course

Rejections will become acceptable, I promise. After a while you get quite blasé about them. And it is only when they begin to pile up that you can call yourself a real author. You have been through the mill, just as well-known authors such as J. K. Rowling have been before you.

The secret is to write, write, write and keep sending your work out. If you have one measly story going the rounds and you sit around biting your nails waiting for an email result, it can be daunting. If you have twenty stories out and get five back – so what? You can live on hope for the other fifteen!

> **MASTERCLASS EXAMPLE**
> Our greatest glory is not in never falling, but in rising every time we fall.
>
> (Confucius)

TOP TIP

If you have posted or emailed your story to a magazine or competition, have another market in mind in case it is rejected. Start thinking *now* how you could alter it to fit another magazine. Then, if the story is rejected, do a rewrite and get it back out there.

LEARNING FROM REJECTION – THE MAIN POINTS
- Rejection is part of the learning process
- Relish – and act upon – any scribbled comments added to the rejection
- The more stories (or novels) you send out, the more chance you have of exchanging rejection slips for acceptances

Exercise 1

Have you any rejected material stashed away in a filing cabinet or on computer? Perhaps a story you were so disappointed about at the time that you couldn't bear to look at it again. Now, after a gap in time, take another look. Could you rewrite it for another market?

Exercise 2

Select a published short story or novel and study the beginning. Jot down some notes as to why you think that story or book was accepted. In what way did it hook the editor?

(47)
WRITING FROM
PERSONAL EXPERIENCE

Most of the fiction we write is from personal experience. We take what we have learned from life – joyful and traumatic events – and use it in our stories. We are confident about doing that, because we feel the story is more likely to work if the events actually happened to us. We can also learn from other people's experience.

Authors such as Melvyn Bragg admit that a lot of their fiction is based on personal experience. Yet others feel happier writing in a genre that is way out of their own comfort zone. Richmal Crompton, with her classic 'Just William' books, achieved great success writing for children, yet never had children of her own. Some excel in the fantasy or science fiction categories and Tracy Chevalier, author of the historical novel *Girl with a Pearl Earring*, says she writes mostly in genres that take her right away from herself and her lifestyle.

Using your own experience
If you want to write contemporary fiction, often the best way is to use your personal experience. And that, of course, cannot always consist of massive, dramatic happenings such as war, murder, massacres and the like. Most ordinary people are never going to go through most of those things, thank heavens. But you can use anything at all that you have learned – how to cope emotionally, how best to react to certain situations, how to curb your temper or cope with an exacting job. And you may prefer to write from experience in this way, using it as a trigger for your imagination; it is, after all, familiar territory.

There are also the events you hear about on the radio, TV, film or read in newspapers. They could be small unimportant things happening to unimportant people, but nevertheless they can spark ideas for plots. The late author, Beryl Bainbridge, said that most of her ideas came from facts in newspapers.

Be observant

Anything you experience is possible material for your writing. That red-faced child screaming in Marks & Spencer – don't just groan, observe her reactions, and her mother's, and *write them down*. Every human problem can be the trigger that sparks off a plot. That teenager grunting down his mobile phone on the bus, the young couple yelling at each other in the supermarket. Recently, I witnessed the rare sight of a child who would not look up from a book to eat his lunch. Not a mobile – a book! Unusual, these days. Remember, though, that you cannot always take events and happenings straight from life. You are writing fiction, so your observations will probably need changing around somewhat. If you can, develop those ideas while they are still 'hot'; there at the front of your mind. (See (2) 'Finding and Recognising Ideas')

Characters

Make it a rule never to use real people in your fiction. That is, don't take them straight from real life, with no changes, etc. In a writing class, if someone reads out a manuscript and the other students remark that the character is lifeless, what follows is predictable. 'But he is my Uncle Ken!' exclaims the author. 'He's real!' And that is why he is lifeless in the story. Using real people in fiction is not a good idea. Apart from the fact that if anything derogatory is said about them they can sue, ordinary people are usually just that – too ordinary – to come to life in a story. Something always needs to be altered or added to make them more interesting. You have to ensure that you have created someone who is perhaps exaggerated and larger than life, yet still credible.

In real life people do odd things, often for reasons we cannot understand. But we shrug and accept those things – he is just a bit odd, we say. Truth is, indeed, stranger than fiction! However, put that odd person into a story and she might not be accepted, unless you give her real motivation for acting like that. Readers like surprises in their fiction, but they do want more valid reasons and explanations than they would expect in real life.

Mundane lives

Some writers say their lives are so mundane that there is no way they could use them to make interesting fiction. Don't ever think that! It is what you do with that knowledge that counts. There is no reason why the circus acrobat, who has toured all over the world and had numerous affairs and traumas over the years, should write a better work of fiction based on personal experience than the shy office cleaner with no family or friends. With a vivid imagination and some twists and turns, who knows what that cleaner could write? It is the treatment of the material that counts. In the same way, think of the jobs, holidays, hobbies, etc., you've had. Try asking 'what if' or 'supposing' ... then change the facts around and fictionalise them.

MASTERCLASS EXAMPLE
The writer's problem is how to strike the balance between the uncommon and the ordinary, so as on the one hand to give interest and on the other to give reality.

(Thomas Hardy)

TOP TIP
If something traumatic has happened in your life, don't try to write about it immediately. Leave a gap in time, or the writing could be over-emotional and too self-indulgent.

WRITING FROM PERSONAL EXPERIENCE – THE MAIN POINTS
• Keep a notebook handy on all occasions

- Don't take people or experiences directly from life. Fictionalise them!
- Twist that mundane event and get a story from it

Exercise 1
What did you do yesterday? Whatever – even if you were ill in bed and did nothing – develop it into an idea for a story.

Exercise 2
What do you consider is the most important thing that has happened to you? Write it down. Now, using that event as a basis, fictionalise the characters and the place and develop it into a structured short story.

(48)
CHECKING ON
MARKET STUDY

If you are writing to sell, market study is vital. If you don't do it you are unlikely to sell your work, unless sheer luck plays a part. Short stories and novels each require a different type of market study, but it is essential in both forms of fiction. If you want to get into print, you must be aware of what is currently selling. Publications such as *The Writers' Handbook* (Macmillan) and the *Writers' and Artists' Year Book* (A & C Black) are a great help, in that they can guide you towards the right market, together with addresses, websites, etc. But make sure you study the very latest editions; markets are changing all the time. Writing magazines – which you can buy in most newsagents and some bookshops – will also keep you up to date with the latest information, such as those publications about to close or merge, plus competitions. But you will need to delve even deeper.

The short story

Women's magazines are the main markets for short stories today. Some authors, having written an emotional story about relationships, tend to pick one such magazine at random and just send off the manuscript. They then wonder why the story comes back. The fact is that you really need to tailor your story specifically for the target publication, then rewrite it before you send it out again.

Why are some writers reluctant to do market study? OK, it can get boring, reading and rereading other people's work. But it is part of the job; an essential part. Ignore it and you will just waste your own time and the editor's, plus postage, if sent by 'snail-mail'. Say you were a food rep, selling sausages. You wouldn't dream of trying to sell them to a fashion store, would you? Of course not! You would research the food markets thoroughly and make a beeline for the one likely to take your brand. So why are writers often so casual about research? However good or original your work, if it does not suit his magazine the editor will reject it. He knows exactly what his readers want and will only accept that type of fiction. If you want to sell your story, it is up to you to fit that format.

Some writers hate the word 'format' – they want to write what they wish, in their own individual style. But often you can still do that – you just have to be willing to 'bend' a little, to suit the magazine. There are so few markets today that, if you want to sell, this is the only way. Having a book of your own short stories published is an unlikely option, unless you are a well-established author. On the bright side, there is always the self-publishing route, if it appeals.

But don't dismiss magazine markets before you've even looked at them. If you can write well, it is such a pity not to have your stuff out there for people to enjoy. Also, though you won't make a fortune, you could be losing out on 'a nice little earner'. Once you are 'in', your name will be registered and your work will no longer be relegated to the magazine's slush pile.

Market research

After you have looked at the writers' market guideline books, go out and buy the magazine you feel you could write for. It is the best and only way to pick up the 'tone'. (More about tone later.) If, after reading it, you still feel it is the right one for you, go on to buy several weeks' issues. You will need up-to-date copies, *not* the ones you find in dentists' and doctors' waiting rooms. Magazines are changing all the time. Study the adverts – which tell you so much about the type of readers – also the articles, readers' letters, the agony column, everything! In particular, you need to research the age group. What type of readers are they? Professional people who play golf, supermarket workers, mothers who enjoy Bingo? What are their problems and hobbies; do they have young children? All this helps so much when you are plotting a story to suit.

And what the actual magazine gives you that other sources cannot is *tone*. It is difficult to put 'tone' into words, but read enough copies and you will get it – the magic essence that makes that publication different. The tone will then automatically come across in your story and you will be well on the way to an acceptance. As well as their weekly editions, most women's magazines publish monthly 'Fiction Specials'. Look out for these – each will give you a whole range of stories in their particular style.

Essential, and enormously helpful, are the magazine's guidelines, available online or by post. Look up the website, which will usually give you bang up-to-date information. Some publications, unfortunately, will not consider manuscripts from writers unknown to them – others welcome new writers. If you study the magazine's requirements before you begin to write you will save yourself a lot of time and disappointment.

Check whether your proposed market prefers you to use email or post. For example, I am aware of one magazine editor who currently ignores anything via email; she will only read manuscripts sent by post. If you are unaware of facts like this, you could be awaiting a decision for ever, because there is no way of knowing whether the editor has deleted your email and your precious manuscript along with it.

Competitions

Further options, for writers who hate the idea of 'format' writing, are short story competitions. You will find plenty of these advertised, both online and in writing magazines. Usually they are 'open'; anything of any category is welcome – sci fi, romance, murder, mystery, historical. You could be lucky with your quirky, different type of story. But always do some research. Read winning entries from earlier competitions; they are often displayed online and they will give you a good idea of the type of story that wins. Also, keep within the required word length or you could be disqualified.

The novel

Did you think about genres before you started your novel? Does yours come under the thriller category, romance, sci fi or historical? You are far more likely to sell it if booksellers can put it under such a 'label'.

Haunt the bookshops, libraries and the internet to see what type of book within your chosen genre is popular at the moment. Not that you'd dream of copying anyone's style or plot (and would have absolutely no chance if you did) but you do need to study the latest trends. The snag with this is that you cannot predict exactly what might be the upcoming fashion in the next year or so. If your book is accepted and takes a while to come out, things will have changed again. If only we could predict these things ...

Market study is just as important with novels – picking a publisher at random is a waste of time. (I once discovered that, prior to coming to my class, one of my students had started the process of sending his novel to *all* the publishers in the *Writers and Artists' Year Book*. He was already about a third of the way through the 'A's'.)

You need to look at the websites of publishers to get an up-to-date feel of what they are looking for. Send for their guidelines and latest catalogues. An increasing number of publishers will now not consider novels unless sent in by an agent. This is frustrating for writers – do they try to get an agent first? It is usually better if you can, because an agent is in a position to know which publisher is looking for what at that time. But the irony is that it can be very difficult to get one to take you on. So the process can become a vicious circle.

Submitting

Most publishers prefer to see your first three chapters, plus the synopsis, rather than the complete novel. If they are interested, they will then ask you to send the rest of the manuscript. Keep your covering letter brief and to the point. Say why you wrote the book, why you think it will sell, what is different about it and tell them of any previous publishing success. Cut all personal comments and let the manuscript speak for itself.

Records

Always keep a record of where you sent the manuscript and the date you sent the material. A card system is fine, or you can keep a record on computer. When accepted or rejected, write down the date. Then, when you send anything else to that publisher, you will have a rough idea how long they take to come to a decision. Keep a record of acceptances, what they paid and when. When you get a rejection, give yourself a boost by getting any acceptance cards out: *'Ah, but I can do it! Here's proof!'*

MASTERCLASS EXAMPLE

A commissioning editor at any large publishing house will receive dozens of manuscripts, all perfectly competent, all sent in by literary agents, every month. If she's to acquire your book, that editor will need to champion it to others in the firm. She needs to build support across the departments: in editorial, in sales, in marketing. That's a tough job and you need to do all you can to help her. No sales director is going to go all gooey inside because you've got a lovely prose style.

(from *How to Write* by Harry Bingham)

TOP TIP

Take a short story from the magazine you wish to write for and copy it, word for word. Writing it out is an excellent way of acquiring that elusive 'tone'. Then delete or destroy your copy.

CHECKING ON MARKET STUDY – THE MAIN POINTS
- Study your proposed market thoroughly
- The editor will not change the style of his magazine to suit your 'masterpiece'
- Read your chosen publisher's latest books, the ones written in your genre

Exercise 1

Select the latest copy of the magazine you intend to write for. Take a sheet of paper (or do it on computer) and divide it into 6 columns. Head them: PLOT, CHARACTERS, DIALOGUE, SETTING, VIEWPOINT, TONE. Underneath each write a few lines about the selected story. For instance, under VIEWPOINT: *From the girl's angle all way through, because it is her story.* TONE: *Gentle, yet sharp writing, with a modern feel about it.*

Exercise 2

Select a book in your chosen genre. Analyse the story and compare it with your own plot. Is yours going to be strong enough, explicit enough, sexy enough? Have you used too many characters or too few?

(49)
REWRITING TO IMPROVE YOUR STORY

How much rewriting do you do? By rewriting I don't mean cutting a few surplus words, adding a bit of essential description or sharpening up some dialogue. I mean do you sometimes have to drastically alter the whole manuscript; changing great chunks or rewriting most of it?

Your own instinct is important and often it is the only thing to go by. You can write the first draft of an entire novel, moving the plot and characters forward as planned, yet know, at the back of your mind, that something is not working. You haven't a clue what it is. But, quite rightly, you press on, because your main aim is to get the story down. Getting that first draft out of the way is crucial. And often it is only through the process of writing that you learn what is wrong with it. So long as you are prepared to rewrite afterwards to improve it, just keep going.

Some warning signs that may mean a rewrite

Problem	What you could do about it
You are writing from a character's viewpoint in the third person and he isn't coming to life.	*What about changing to the first person (still tell the story from his angle, but in the 'I' viewpoint)?*
Nothing seems to be happening, though your original plot seemed exciting enough.	*If the story is not moving, either in a dramatic or emotional way, you are going to have to change it so that it does.*

Problem	What you could do about it
You are bored with your characters.	*Good characterisation is vital and a complete revamp of your characters will alter the whole tone of the story.*
The pace feels too slow for the adventure genre you are writing for.	*Does the plot need 'jazzing' up? Maybe the time sequence is wrong?*
If it is a short story, is it confusing?	*Have you used too many characters? Are you trying to cram too much into 2,000 words? Alternatively, is the plot too thin to stretch to 2,000 words?*
You've tried reading it aloud to your local writers' group and found the different comments contradictory.	*If just two of the more experienced writers said the same (predictable plot, wooden characters, or whatever) pounce on that.*

Major rewriting

Any of the above factors will probably mean a major rewrite. It won't be just a matter of 'cut and paste', but an overhaul of the whole story. If, when you reach the end of the first draft, you still cannot see what is wrong, put the manuscript away and forget about it for a week or two. Write something else. Then take another look. Hopefully, coming back to it 'cold', the faults will jump out … and you will be faced with a lot of rewriting. Quite an undertaking, especially if it is a novel. But well worth doing if you believe in the story.

Whether you will have to do a hatchet job and delete the whole original story depends on your findings – maybe if it's a character flaw you can put that right throughout the original manuscript. But do reread the entire story – it is surprising how, say, a character's changed attitude can affect the smallest details. The way people speak, for instance. Supposing you have created your character, Liz, as a gentle soul at the beginning of your novel but by the end she is quite vicious. You have realised that will not work – the reader will not believe in her changing so drastically by the end. So you have to do a rewrite, making her less gentle at the start.

Example (first draft):

'Liz, would you take Maisie out for me, please?' Mum said.

Liz sighed. Dog-walking was not one of her favourite things, but then Mum was not well.

'Course I will,' she said cheerily.

Example (second draft):

'Liz, would you take Maisie out for me, please?' Mum said.

Liz sighed, irritated. She hated dog-walking. Mum not being well was a bit of a pain.

'In a minute,' she muttered.

And, of course, there would be other ways to hint at Liz's underlying nature throughout the story. Note the earlier warning about checking the whole story for any essential rewrites. Supposing you decided to change viewpoint from third person to first. Merely changing all the 'he's' to 'I's' will not suffice. An 'I' viewpoint will alter the whole concept of the story and the tone, as well as the main character.

If an editor or publisher suggests a rewrite, do it. You may feel indignant at first, thinking this is your baby, but they know the market better than you do and are aware what will suit your book and sell more copies. Also, when you eventually do the alterations, you will no doubt be surprised how the story has improved. Should you still feel you have a valid point in objecting, however, get an experienced writer's opinion before you contact the publisher. Sometimes you are too close to the story yourself to see where you have gone wrong.

> **MASTERCLASS EXAMPLE**
> There is no great writing, only great rewriting.
>
> (Justice Brandeis)

TOP TIP

Even if you don't feel your manuscript warrants rewriting, go back and look again at the beginning. This is the first example of your writing the publisher sees. It needs to be spot on.

REWRITING TO IMPROVE YOUR STORY – THE MAIN POINTS

- If you have doubts about a particular piece, it probably needs a rewrite
- If characterisation or viewpoint rewrites are required, reread the whole story
- If you are aware that the story does not work but cannot see why, put the manuscript away for a few weeks and then look at it again

Exercise 1

Rewrite the following passage of dialogue. At the moment it is all rather cosy and dull; make it sharper, more emotional. Does it start at the right place?

'Hello, Eileen! Nice to see you. Have a cup of tea?'

'Yes, please, Kay.'

'You don't look very happy. Have a biscuit?'

'No, thanks.'

Eileen burst into tears.

'Whatever is wrong, Eileen? You are usually so cheerful. How is Tom?'

'Actually, he left me yesterday,' she sniffed.

'Oh, dear! Would you like a tissue?'

'Yes, please, Kay.'

Exercise 2

Take one of your rejected stories and study one page (preferably the first). Go through it meticulously and rewrite the whole page, cutting, sharpening, tightening it up ruthlessly and bringing it up to date. Does it read better? Now do the same with the whole story.

(50)
BEING ECONOMICAL
WITH WORDS

Have you ever written a story for a market or competition and found you are 300 words or so over the required length? At first you despair: 300 words to cut! It will mean drastically altering the whole story. Then you begin the process … and the number of words you find you can get rid of without 'losing the plot' is frightening! Why, you wonder, were they there in the first place? When you have finished, you find you have tightened and improved the writing tremendously.

The aim is to make every word count – essential in a short story with its length limits, but just as vital in a novel. The difficulty, especially for beginners, is in knowing exactly where to cut and how much. Strip your writing right down and the danger is that you could lose some of the best bits – the essence of the story, the sensory aspects such as smell, taste, etc., or background. The more writing you do, the more you will learn to balance this – you will keep the essentials, but discard any surplus words or material.

Cutting useless words
Let's begin with a list of words which, when cut, can add so much to the sharpness of the writing:

very	almost	nearly
quite	rather	slightly
fairly	somewhat	basically
just	really	seem

Using any of the above can weaken the sentence and muffle the meaning.

For instance, take the word 'just':

He just couldn't understand a word of it.

Or, simply:

He couldn't understand a word of it.

Now the word 'really':

You really shouldn't swear like that.

Or, simply:

You shouldn't swear like that.

Cut words such as 'the', 'a' or 'an', to give stronger impact. *Traffic whizzed by,* instead of *The traffic whizzed by. Sadness hit her* instead of *A wave of sadness hit her.*

Redundant words

Watch out for phrases containing redundant words (in italics):

He sat down *on the seat* (where else would he sit?)

A frown appeared *on her face* (where else?)

He nodded *his head* (what else?)

He held a gun *in his hand* (where else?)

She shrugged *her shoulders* (what else)

Do you need the words in italics in these phrases:

the sky *above*	a *cold* chill	a *little* baby
a *brief* glance	each *and every*	gather *together*
whether *or not*	*end* result	a *terrible* muddle

Sentences

Streamlining your sentences and varying the length of them will improve your work. But economy in writing does not necessarily mean always keeping sentences short. Often the rhythm of the writing is improved by varying the sentence length. Having said that, you will often need to divide very long sentences into two, for reasons of economy and clarity.

Adjectives, adverbs and clichés

Cut as many as possible. For example: *Her thin cotton jumper.* The double adjectives in that sentence tell us absolutely nothing – if it is cotton we guess that it is thin. *Her green cotton jumper* would have been better, so we could visualise it. Adverbs (words that end in 'ly') are often surplus: *He slammed the phone down forcefully* or *She stormed angrily out of the room.* In both those cases the adverbs are unnecessary because the verbs have done the work. (See (37) 'Using Adjectives and Adverbs'.)

Clichés, apart from those used in dialogue, must be avoided: *She was grasping at straws. He was a real wet blanket. Her hands were cold as ice.* Find your own original description, if you can.

Study the following paragraph and see whether you agree that all the words in italics could be cut:

The *rays of the* sun burned Tilly's skin as she walked across the *open* field to get to the *busy* main road *and the top of the hill* to reach the shops. She usually met Pam and Julie for lunch *at twelve o'clock*, but today they could only make it for coffee, so they were meeting earlier, *at eleven.* Tilly stopped *for a minute,* got out her bottle of water, *unscrewed the top* and drank greedily. Phew, it was *so baking hot,* a real scorcher *today.*

Dialogue and repetition

Is every word of your dialogue necessary? Dialogue is not there just to look pretty on the page, but to aid characterisation and to move the story on. Check that it is not repetitious or rambling:

Now she knew she was pregnant, Kelly would have liked to keep the news to herself for a bit, but realised that would be impossible. For a start, there was the morning sickness so Jane, at work, needed to be told before she guessed.

'Jane, I've something to tell you,' she said at work the next morning.

'Oh? Got promotion?'

'No. Actually, I'm pregnant.'

Jane stared, then burst out laughing.

'Don't believe it! You, a mum with a bawling baby. What a hoot!'

Kelly sighed. She might have known Jane would react like this …

Did we need that conversation? The reader already knew about Kelly's pregnancy so does not need to hear about it again. In this case the dialogue is not moving the story on. All we need is: *When she got to work next morning and told Jane, Jane burst out laughing.* Otherwise you are in danger of boring the reader. Direct dialogue there would only be justified if Jane was a really important character and her reaction was crucial to the story. Maybe if Kelly was pregnant by Jane's ex-boyfriend? Then the repetition would be justified.

Check for repetition of obvious words close to each other and change them. In the first draft, you are usually just getting the story down, so it is easy to repeat yourself. And never try to be clever with long words or expressions you think will impress. They won't – they'll just irritate readers who are only interested in the story and how it progresses.

> **MASTERCLASS EXAMPLE**
>
> From inside he heard the bleating of a terminally wounded saxophone. Doc had ideas about music different from most people's.
>
> 'Been a while,' Driver said when the door opened to a nose like a bloated mushroom, soft-poached eyes.
>
> 'Seems like just yesterday,' Doc said. 'Course, to me everything seems like just yesterday. When I remember it at all.'
>
> Then he just stood there. The sax went on bleating behind him.
>
> (from *Drive* by James Sallis)

TOP TIP

The word 'then' is often overused by writers. In fiction, one event follows another anyway – readers expect it. So *Then she decided to …* is unnecessary. Just *She decided to …*

BEING ECONOMICAL WITH WORDS – THE MAIN POINTS
- Be ruthless and sharpen your writing by cutting every 'very', 'almost', 'nearly' and the like
- Cut adjectives, adverbs, clichés
- Check for repetition of words, also content. Does the reader already know that fact?

Exercise 1

Tighten up the following paragraph, concentrating on economy of words and content.

Celia had very nearly fallen down outside the busy bookshop. She almost tripped on her patent leather high-heels and the blonde shop assistant had quickly hurried outside to see that she was all right. Celia seemed somewhat shaky and attempted to sit down on the wet, dirty pavement but the helpful girl assistant hurriedly went back inside and fetched a chair. Thankfully, Celia sat down on it.

Exercise 2

Take a published short story and analyse it. Could you tighten it to make the writing sharper? If that particular one is faultless, choose another and strike out words you feel are unnecessary. How many words would you have cut?

LIST OF CREDITS

Pat Barker *Double Vision* First published by Penguin Books Ltd., 2003 (© Pat Barker)

H. E. Bates *The Fabulous Mrs V.* First published by Michael Joseph, 1964. Reproduced by permission of Pollinger Limited and Tim Bates

James Scott Bell *Plot & Structure* Published by Writers' Digest Books, F+W Media, 2004

Harry Bingham *How To Write* First published by Bloomsbury Publishing Plc, 2012

William Boyd *Restless* First published by Bloomsbury Publishing Plc, 2006

Tracy Chevalier *Girl With a Pearl Earring* First published by Harper Collins Publishers Ltd., 1999

Margaret Forster *The Unknown Bridesmaid* Published by Chatto & Windus, 2013

Alison Gibbs *Writers on Writing* (P. D. James' comment) Published by Robert Hale Ltd., 1995

Lesley Glaister *The Private Parts of Women* (© Lesley Glaister). First published by Bloomsbury Publishing Plc., 1996. Reprinted by permission of A. M. Heath & Co. Ltd.

Winston Graham *The Walking Stick* (© Winston Graham). First published by Collins,1967. Reprinted by permission of A. M. Heath & Co. Ltd.

Graham Greene *Brighton Rock* Published by Vintage Books, 2004. Reprinted by permission of David Higham Associates

Jennifer Johnston *How Many Miles to Babylon?* First published by Hamish Hamilton, 1974. Reprinted by permission of David Higham Associates

Lars Kepler *The Hypnotist* Reprinted by permission of HarperCollins Publishers Ltd., 2009

Francis King 'A Nice Way to Go' from *Hard Feelings and Other Stories* First published by Hutchinson & Co. Ltd., 1976 (© Francis King). Reprinted by permission of A. M. Heath & Co. Ltd.

Maggie O'Farrell *After You'd Gone* (© Maggie O'Farrell). First published by Review (Headline Book Publishing), 2000. Reprinted by permission of A. M. Heath & Co. Ltd.

James Sallis *Drive* First published by No Exit Press, 2005

Sue Townsend *The Woman Who Went To Bed for a Year* First published by Michael Joseph, 2012 – an imprint of Penguin Books. Reproduced by permission of Curtis Brown Ltd.

Louise Welsh *The Bullet Trick,* 2002. Reproduced by permission of the author c/o Rogers, Coleridge & White Ltd.

Every effort has been made to obtain the necessary permissions with reference to copyright material, both illustrative and quoted. We apologise for any omissions in this respect and will be pleased to make the appropriate acknowledgements in any future edition.

INDEX